$\mathscr{M}$ORE THAN
PETTICOATS

———◦►◄◦———

REMARKABLE
WISCONSIN
$\mathscr{W}$OMEN

MORE THAN PETTICOATS SERIES

MORE THAN PETTICOATS

REMARKABLE WISCONSIN WOMEN

Greta Anderson

TWODOT®

GUILFORD, CONNECTICUT
HELENA, MONTANA
AN IMPRINT OF THE GLOBE PEQUOT PRESS

A · TWODOT® · BOOK

Cover photo: The Ingenues girls band members serenading cows at the University of Wisconsin Dairy Barn, Madison, August 6, 1930. Courtesy Wisconsin Historical Society.

Text design: Cyndee Peil

Library of Congress Cataloging-in-Publication Data
Anderson, Greta.
    More than petticoats : remarkable Wisconsin women / Greta Anderson.
       p. cm.-- (More than petticoats series)
    Includes bibliographical references and index.
    Contents: Queen Marinette -- Eliza Chappell Porter -- Cordelia P. Harvey -- Margarethe Meyer Schurz -- Belle Case La Follette – Harriet Bell Merrill -- Lillie Rosa Minoka-Hill -- Elsa Ulbricht -- Edna Ferber -- Mabel Watson Raimey -- Golda Meir -- Mildred Fish-Harnack.
    ISBN 0-7627-2529-X
    1. Women–Wisconsin–Biography. 2. Women–Wisconsin–History.
    3. Wisconsin–Biography. I. Title. II. Series.

CT3262.W6A53 2004
920.082'775--dc22
                                                    2004047337

Manufactured in the United States of America
First Edition/First Printing

Dedicated to the young women of Wisconsin

$\mathscr{C}$ONTENTS

ACKNOWLEDGMENTS

Any book of history is written, as the saying goes, "standing on the shoulders of giants." Therefore, I first thank those individuals whose dedicated research and writing enabled my storytelling: Shareen Blair Brysac (Mildred Fish-Harnack), Roberta Jean Hill (Lillie Rosa Minoka-Hill), Merrilyn L. Hartridge (Harriet Bell Merrill), Beverly Hayward Johnson (Queen Marinette), Phoebe Weaver Williams (Mabel Watson Raimey), and Lucy Freeman, Sherry La Follette, and George Zabriskie (Belle Case La Follette). Their work was indispensable in my understanding of their respective subjects, and I happily recommend their work to readers who wish to delve deeper.

Albert Muchka and Phoebe Williams provided personal assistance on the chapter on Mabel Watson Raimey. I thank them warmly.

I also thank Arlene Sand, Interlibrary Loan Specialist at the Kirkwood Community College library in Cedar Rapids, for her cheerful assistance in locating books. Thanks also to Sue Leibold on the Iowa City end of the book relay.

My editors at Globe Pequot deserve thanks for their professionalism, patience, and encouraging words: Megan Hiller, Stephanie Hester, Patricia Meyers, and Amy Hrycay each contributed significantly to readying the manuscript for publication.

Finally, I owe a great debt to my father, Jon Mac Anderson, not only for his expert editing of each chapter herein, but also for much inspiration in my development as a writer. I believe it was in his editing of my junior high American history essays that I first began to appreciate the logic and precision of the English language.

All of these have contributed significantly to the strengths of the book. Whatever failings it has are my own.

INTRODUCTION

In his 1840 lectures on heroes, Thomas Carlyle stated that "History is at bottom the history of Great Men." This series extends that notion to women. It also questions the notion of what constitutes "greatness." Could it include great sympathy and understanding, great vision, great commitment, great risks, as well as great undertakings? I believe it can, and I wouldn't put it past Carlyle, either. For all his hero-worship, he was mainly interested in *inspiration* and the question, whence come those forces that move people, together, in directions that change the course of history.

I wrote these biographies to inspire, but also to present a *text* of nineteenth through twentieth century Wisconsin history. For one can probably learn more about history, especially social history—the *texture* of a historic time—from reading a group of women's biographies than from a similar group of men's biographies. Men's action, or perhaps simply the stories told about it, often seems divorced from its social context. Women's action is more often negotiated in relation to the times, especially in relation to the prevailing views of marriage, family, and work. The threads of history, the warp and weft of ideas, individuals, and institutions, run through these lives to create a patterned *textile* of history.

Numerous people have asked how I selected the subjects in this book. There is no simple formula, and the choices were in some cases very difficult to make. The books in the "More than Petticoats" series have several things in common. They are composed of factual, readable biographies representing women who are diverse in terms of their backgrounds and accomplishments and their residence within a particular state. All are born before 1900.

(In the case of Mildred Fish-Harnack, though, my editors allowed me to "cheat.") There are women from northeast Wisconsin, Green Bay, Milwaukee, Madison, southeast Wisconsin, and Portage. These women are doctors, lawyers, businesswomen, politicians, scientists, and authors. They are Menominee, German-American, Scots-Irish, Yankee, Mohawk, African-American, and Jewish.

Other factors enter in, of course. First, a woman's life must have sufficient documentation to create a biography that is factual. This is a significant barrier in writing about women of the past, especially about minority women. Second, the woman's life must make a good story. There must be action, and, preferably, it should be set in Wisconsin. There should be conflict and resolution to the action, and it should be historically significant. Third, the story that I wish to tell must be significantly different from the stories my sources have told—either in terms of audience, format, theme, or accessibility.

Finally, and perhaps most importantly, I strive to feel a personal connection with the subject. All women's lives are unique, but as I've suggested, common threads run through them. A woman of forty, as I am, has taken up many of these threads, has dropped some, gotten tangled in others, and used some of them as lifelines to find a place in the world. In writing each biography I sought out that connection, that common thread, then began to explore my subject's choices and struggles from the vantage point of my own self-knowledge. In this sense, writing biographies is similar to acting.

In any collection of remarkable women, the question of marriage will emerge. This was particularly true of Wisconsin women. Several of the women deliberately chose not to marry. Others discovered themselves through their husbands' lives or work; most faced struggles about their commitments and identities. Although today's women have many more opportunities than those of the past, the conflict between love and career remains a theme in our lives, much more so than in men's.

Other common themes seem to reflect on the particularity of Wisconsin as a state. Wisconsin's progressive vein of politics is well represented by Belle Case La Follette and others. I found it interesting, also, how Elsa Ulbricht, Mabel Watson Raimey, and Golda Meir all grew up virtually within the same area of Milwaukee. As they are of German, African, and Jewish descent, their lives speak to the historic diversity of that city and to the stimulating effect that diversity has on individuals. Other major themes in Wisconsin history include education and experimentation—often in combination. In addition, the state has retained some of its connections to Native culture and stories. It has been a great font of women writers, and was a great enemy of the Nazis.

For me, the journey through time and space to "meet" these women and imagine their lives has been a fascinating one. I hope you will feel the same when you read this collection of biographies.

QUEEN
MARINETTE
1793–1865

Matriarch of the Menominee

*S*o the American, Farnsworth, had left her for a business prospect elsewhere. Perhaps he would come back; perhaps he wouldn't. Did it matter? What can you say of a man who, after twelve years of partnership, refuses to claim you as his wife, even when you are carrying his third child? A man who treats your people as if they were mere obstacles to his designs—even when they had been the very basis of his business?

At the age of thirty-nine, Marinette retained her youthful beauty—the long rope of silky black hair, strong cheekbones, dark eyes, the hint of a smile at the corners of her mouth. She might again find a man if she needed one. But, while it is true that they had given her six healthy children and established her in the trading business, both of her partners had proved more trouble than they were worth. A smile crept into the corners of Marinette's mouth. To her, the trading post had always been a way of life, not only for herself but for the people of the region. Now she could run the post and lead her community exactly as she wished.

More than Petticoats

* * *

Marinette was a born trader, coming from a family of French and Menominee mixed-blood traders named Chevalier. The family's fur trading activities can be traced back to her great-great-grandfather Jean-Baptiste Chevalier, who traded out of Montreal in the late 1600s. Most of these ancestors married Menominee or *metis* (mixed-blood) women or, as in the case of Marinette's father, a full-blood Chippewa. Marinette's maternal grandfather was a Chippewa chief called Ke-che-waub-ish-ashe, or "Big Marten," a tribal hero who died in battle against the Chippewa's longtime foe, the Sioux. The Chippewa and the Menominee and their French brothers got along well; Marinette's mixed lineage was not unusual on the Wisconsin frontier.

Earlier Chevaliers traded out of Fort Michilimackinac, on the straits of Mackinac where Lake Michigan joins Lake Huron in a system of waterways that ultimately reaches Hudson Bay and the Atlantic Ocean. As a young man, Marinette's grandfather moved to "Le Baie" at the mouth of the Fox River. This settlement was tied into the Upper Mississippi trade route as well as the Great Lakes routes. At that time, Green Bay was sending out hundreds of packet-boats a year and ranked among the top three posts, though the beaver population was beginning to decline. When Marinette was a young woman, beaver would become locally extinct and muskrats become the standard catch.

Winter was the prime hunting season, when the animal's coats were the thickest and they could be seen against the snow. Marinette's father, Bathelemy, would spend the season at his northern camp on Post Lake, sometimes bringing his family with him. There, he would gather pelts and hides from the Indians in exchange for European goods such as blankets and cookware. According to legend, it was at the outpost that Marinette was born, around 1793. When not in winter quarters, the family lived on the Fox River near present-day De Pere. Summers were spent gathering wild rice and berries, fishing, growing crops, and making the short trip into Le Baie. The community was racially diverse but closely knit. Marinette would have had many relatives in the area.

On the American frontier and especially in Indian cultures, girls age fourteen were considered marriageable. Sometime between 1807 and 1810, Jean-Baptiste Jacobs, newly arrived from Montreal, saw the young Marinette, decided that he wanted her for his wife, and approached her father with his proposal. Jacobs had prosperous relatives in Le Baie but no particular plans in life beyond inheriting his father's estate when his older brother died. However, his handwriting was impeccable and he spoke both French and English fluently. He must have seemed to be a man with decent prospects. The marriage contract was sealed before the local French magistrate.

During the first years of their marriage, Jacobs shuttled back and forth between Le Baie and duties in Canada, the most important of which was to curry favor with his ailing brother. The War of 1812, which pitted the Americans against the French, broke out along the Canadian–American frontier, disrupting travel and trade. Back in Le Baie *"Verte"*—or Green Bay, as it was becoming known—Marinette was kept busy with successive pregnancies and childbirths. She probably had the full attention of her mother, who had recently been widowed. When Jacobs finally rejoined Marinette in 1820, their family included two daughters and a son. Jacobs made a half-hearted attempt to start a French school, then found brief employment as a trading clerk for one of his Green Bay relatives but was dismissed when he "abandoned scruples" regarding three kegs of whiskey he was supposed to deliver. In 1822 he finally wrested the promise of the inheritance he sought from his brother and also landed a post with the American Fur Company at the mouth of the Menominee River.

The War of 1812 had changed the fur trade forever. The Americans, whose victory established their claim to the region, were much more aggressive in business than the French had been. While families like the Chevaliers traded for life, the Americans traded for profits, the bigger and faster, the better. The German immigrant John Jacob Astor epitomized this spirit. He amassed a small fortune selling furs in New York City through the 1790s, then started the American Fur Company in 1808. Aided by U.S. law after the War of 1812, he expelled the foreign competition, bought off local officials, obtained a monopoly, and, in 1834, by then a multimillionaire, sold the business and sank the proceeds into real estate, three years before the Panic of 1837 caused markets to collapse.

Marinette's trader husband was not an American and did not act like one. Though he could read and write two languages, he left practically all the work and bookkeeping of the Menominee River post to his young wife. Though illiterate, she was fluent in the oral Ojibway/Chippewa language of trade and kept excellent records using the pictographs she had learned from her father. In the late fall up to forty hunters would enter her trading post to reckon for goods they would need at their hunting grounds. Marinette drove a fair bargain, tallied credit, and made friendly conversation with them all. The Menominee quickly warmed to her in this role. Jacobs's competitor across the river, William Farnsworth, noticed all this, and after Jacobs's first season at the Menominee, began to employ his secret weapon, an illegal stash of whiskey, in a scheme to steal this remarkable woman away from her unambitious husband.

Jacobs fell for the bait, sacrificing most of his fur profits to Farnsworth in exchange for the liquor, then relied upon the latter's charity to supply his family with items such as children's clothing. Farnsworth's readiness to help in this way surely caught Marinette's attention. Jacobs then played directly into Farnsworth's hand by inviting him to join their household over the winter of 1822 to 1823. Farnsworth, who had been trading out of a temporary "jack-knife" post, graciously accepted, and by spring, Marinette was his. It was not uncommon for marriages between Native American women and traders to be amicably dissolved, and this was the case with Jacobs and Marinette. Jacobs returned to Montreal with high hopes for his fortune, though he never did inherit what he had assumed would be his birthright.

Farnsworth was emphatically not an American Fur Company agent, and this, as well as the whisky he was known to trade, made it difficult for him to obtain his annual license from the government Indian agents. When he was forced to travel to Mackinack in search of a friendly agent, the Green Bay traders associated with the American Fur Company moved into the vacant post. However, the local Menominees knew with whom they wanted to trade, and as soon as Farnsworth returned in his loaded canoe, they emptied the post of the usurper's goods and installed Farnsworth's. Once Marinette arrived and began to conduct business in her inimitably winning way, the American Fur Company finally conceded the site and established their man, Chaput, at a post a few miles north.

In addition to her personality, other factors played a role in Marinette's success. American Fur Company agents received trade goods on credit from the firm, extended those goods on credit to the native hunters, then collected furs at the end of the winter and began the cycle again. The company agents as well as the Indians were squeezed by the inflationary tendencies of this credit system, receiving less in goods than seemed fair for a quantity of furs. The independent Green Bay merchant with whom Farnsworth did business shunned credit, dealing only in "cash and carry." Marinette in turn rarely extended credit, and because of this could provide necessary household goods at lower prices than most of her competitors. At the same time, Marinette always welcomed and assisted Menominees or Chippewas in need of practical, personal help.

With Marinette handling most of the details of the trading post, Farnsworth began scheming for a lumber mill along the Menominee River—on valuable land that was by law the Menominees'. The territorial governor finally approved his plan over the objections of the Indian agent. Farnsworth agreed to pay the local Menominee chiefs powder, lead, flints, and pipes from the store, as well as "all the sawn lumber they required" (which, given their style of pole dwellings, amounted to exactly nothing), and ten bushels of corn each, which Marinette supplied from her garden. When it was discovered that the sawmill blocked huge numbers of whitefish from spawning upriver, Farnsworth simply installed a weir and harvested them, as yet another division of his business. All this business created a rift between Farnsworth and Marinette, now the mother of two of his children. His indifference to the death of Joset Caron, the local French Menominee chief, seemed to underscore the exploitative nature of their relationship. He never visited the ailing man, and when relatives asked for clothes in which to bury him, Farnsworth replied, "I ain't got nothing to give him."

Eventually, he gave Caron's relatives a cheap blanket from the store. But for one with deep Menominee roots, as Marinette had, the offense was unforgivable. These were her people. It seems safe to assume that Marinette was not a histrionic woman; however, according to the rival trader Chaput, who deeply respected her, she and her daughter were "crying all the time" following this incident. He added that it appeared that Farnsworth was glad that the concessions he had made to the chief in the sawmill negotiations were no longer in force.

Thus it was that Marinette must have felt a degree of relief when Farnsworth refused for the third and last time to claim her as his wife. The incident occurred between 1833 and 1834, when Marinette was pregnant with their third child. The American Fur Company men in Green Bay always kept a close eye on Farnsworth, the perpetual thorn under their skin. His skillful attorney had so far enabled him to evade their attempts to incriminate him, but when Marinette's condition became obvious, they summoned him to court once again with charges of "fornication." Simply acknowledging her as his wife would have voided the charges; instead, Farnsworth engaged in a more complicated legal sidestep and left to start a new lumber mill in Sheboygan, much closer to the waves of white immigration coming into the region. In 1834, the year Astor left the fur trade, Farnsworth did so as well. His brother Samuel took over the Menominee sawmill, while Marinette and her six children stayed at her post in the little village that would eventually bear her name.

* * *

Times were difficult for the Menominee and the Chippewa in the 1830s and the decades to follow. Businessmen like Astor and Farnsworth had shown little concern for the long-term sustainability of the fur trade. Animals were overhunted and had retreated from regions where commercial logging occurred. The market for furs faced a downturn, as well, due to changes in fashion, and finally collapsed in 1837. At the same time, smallpox, "the white man's disease," descended upon the Menominees. Native Americans everywhere were particularly susceptible to its ravages because they lacked the immunity Europeans had developed over centuries of raising domesticated animals. The Indians in different regions were affected at different times, usually when their contact with white settlers reached a critical mass.

Thus weakened, the Menominee gradually saw their tribal lands taken away from them. In 1836 the U.S. government began negotiations to remove them from their ancestral lands. According to her biographer, Marinette—in her role as a bridge between the white and Indian worlds—helped to postpone the inevitable for a time. However, when Wisconsin became a state in 1848, the campaign to dislodge the Menominees was renewed. Marinette and 300 others elected to sacrifice tribal rights in exchange for a one-time payment; this enabled them to purchase property in their tribal homeland rather than accept arbitrary relocation to a reservation.

During these difficult decades, Marinette was the one to whom others turned for comfort. A contemporary described her as "an excellent neighbor, kind and skillful in cases of sickness and ready to help the distressed." Another contemporary echoed these words: she was "looked to as a mother by all the early settlers and Indians, for she had always been ready to assist the needy and comfort the distressed." This generosity was what her culture taught, both the Native traditions and her French-Catholic faith. Indeed, now that the ambiguity of her relationship to Farnsworth was no longer an impediment, Marinette was properly baptized, as all of her children had been. While she remained, in the eyes of all those who met her, a consummate and even "shrewd" businesswoman, there was none of the stinginess Farnsworth had shown in his dealings with the people. Instead, Marinette showed herself to be adaptable in ways that benefited both her business and her community. In response to the dwindling fur trade, she procured iron kettles, ladles, and molds for local people to use in setting up "sugar camps" to boil maple syrup into cakes for trade. When more white settlers began arriving in the region, she sold them wild rice, cranberries, and fish supplied by local Menominees.

Around 1850 Marinette turned the business over to her eldest son John Jacobs Jr. and returned to the agricultural life of her girlhood, supplying corn to the trading post and planting an extensive apple orchard. Jacobs bought a steamboat, the *Queen City*, to transport passengers, freight, and salted fish between the Menominee and Green Bay. He also built a new two-story trading post to serve as the town's social and business center. The festive occasions held there created fond memories for those who experienced them. Today, it is fascinating to imagine those days when whites and Indians in beaded buckskin attire mingled in almost equal numbers and social status, dancing the French four or quadrille to fiddle music.

By the time Marinette turned the business over, she had become a legend. Her name was given to the city in 1855; the title "Queen" might have arisen first from her association with the steamer but was altogether derived from her status in the community.

Marinette died in 1865 and was buried in the Menominee fashion, in her own backyard, with a cedar log structure above the grave. When the lumber industry came to the town of Marinette in earnest, necessitating the destruction of her home, her remains were moved to the Allouez cemetery in Green Bay, where several of her offspring lived with their families. She is remembered yet today throughout the region.

Eliza Chappell Porter

1807–1888

A Missionary at Heart

From the end of January, through February, and into March of 1834, the twenty-six-year-old Eliza Chappell lay prostrate on her bed, unable to rise. The past year had taxed her energies and emotions. She had traveled throughout the East raising funds, founded a school near Mackinaw, and sailed for the village of Chicago to start another school, where sixty students of different ages now called her their teacher. Twelve of them lived with her, at the request of their parents. And on Sundays the schoolhouse was filled with the singing of hymns, as the church established by the Reverend Jeremiah Porter at Fort Dearborn had, with Eliza's efforts, expanded its mission into the community.

Then, Rev. Porter had proposed marriage. When Eliza rose from her sickbed, she accepted his offer.

Eliza's friends were aghast. Physically, Eliza was a wisp of a woman who gave the impression of being halfway to heaven already. The fact that she bore the hardships of frontier life was miracle enough. But marriage and childbirth! Was she mad? Surely Miss Chappell did not understand the nature of her commitment.

Rev. Porter also received little encouragement from friends, but that did not affect his resolve. Throughout the year he wrote devoted letters to Eliza, expressing his joy at having found someone who so completely shared his life's mission to minister to those at the edge of Western civilization.

When Eliza traveled to New England to meet the reverend's family, it was a study in contrasts. Rev. Porter's mother and sisters were sturdy, energetic women who might have been useful on the frontier. Eliza was frail, even sickly looking: As a side effect of calomel treatments during an illness in adolescence, she had lost nearly all her teeth. One afternoon before the wedding, as the groom's mother and the bride-to-be sat beside one another, Mrs. Porter took Eliza's delicate, translucent hand in her own and exclaimed, almost unconsciously, "Oh! What can such a poor little hand do?"

Eliza did not take offense. She understood her mother-in-law's anguish about her dearest child's future. She only smiled inwardly at the thought that had become so familiar to her: It was not her own strength that she trusted but that of her Lord and Savior. Still, no one could have known how far that strength would carry her.

* * *

Eliza was the youngest daughter in a family of eight children. Her father's death when she was four years old prompted Eliza to become her mother Elizabeth's emotional consort and, as she was able, her helper. The family lived in Geneseo, New York, near Buffalo, but originated from farm country 250 miles away, near the Connecticut border. A prosperous married cousin visiting the Geneseo household took note of the widow's burden and offered to adopt Eliza. The young girl struggled fiercely against this notion and ultimately had her way. She would go to live on their farm, but strictly as a "little cousin."

Eliza thrived indoors and out, learning from her cousin how to cook and spin wool, and competing with the boys in outdoor sports. All the while, though, she thought of her mother, and at age twelve returned to Geneseo with the vow, "Now I will never leave you again." Elizabeth's fervent religious feelings had met only indifference in her other children; her youngest daughter, however, entered fully into Elizabeth's emotional faith—at that time generally associated with the Methodist Church, but in her case with the Presbyterian. In the next few years Eliza "wept, fasted, prayed and studied" herself into a state of precarious health. Her burdens increased when her sister died and left four younger children to her and her mother's care. At age sixteen she took charge of the district school, studying the Bible and other books in her spare moments in order to attain a higher standard of learning and devotion.

Under this regimen, Eliza finally collapsed. For nine months doctors labored over her with their late-1820s medical technologies—cauterization and bloodletting. Lying practically lifeless after this course of treatment, Eliza finally asked her mother to "give her up" to the Lord—to let go of the expectation that she would live to take care of her in old age. This release granted, Eliza felt the life drain out of her. Then, by her account, she reached under her pillow for her Bible and had a very interesting conversation with herself:

"Do you believe the Book is the word of God?"

"Yes!"

"Do you believe every word of it."

"Yes!"

"Will you believe what you now find in that Book as you open it?"

"I will."

Eliza opened to John 11: 25–26: "He that believeth in me though he were dead yet he shall live, and he that liveth and believeth in me shall never die." At that moment Eliza felt she saw flash before her the whole plan of salvation by faith: The purpose of her struggle had been to bring her "to cease from self and rest in Christ alone." She felt unutterable joy; her soul "was melted with intense gratitude and love."

Eliza quit taking her medications. She got out of bed and crept across the floor, each day a bit farther. Then she attempted to walk. When she had regained her strength, she considered her life wholly the Lord's. The following year her mother Elizabeth died. Eliza "buried her dead" and was ready to follow her faith.

The year 1830 was a good time to be "born again." It was the beginning of the Second Great Awakening, a vast evangelical movement in cities across the eastern United States. That year Charles G. Finney, the movement's leader, held revivals in Philadelphia, New York City, and Rochester, New York. Just four months before Elizabeth's death, mother and daughter had moved to Rochester to live with Eliza's brothers, possibly also to participate in Finney's September revival, considered one of his greatest successes. Eliza's dramatic near-death experience became a well-known story in the revival town as she continued her career as a schoolteacher.

Out in the wilderness, another New York resident had undergone conversion. In 1828 Robert Stuart, the partner of fur baron John Jacob Astor and discoverer of the Oregon Trail, "got religion" on Mackinac Island from missionaries (some of whom returned to live in Rochester) and desired to serve God while still on Astor's payroll there. When it was learned that the Stuarts needed a teacher for their children, the Rochester missionaries wrote them of the exciting new arrival, Miss Eliza Chappell.

Eliza's ready decision to join the couple in Mackinaw brought out the protests of her skeptical friends and family, who thought such a post eminently unsuitable for an invalid such as she. Nonetheless, she arrived safely after several weeks of travel. The home of the Stuarts, who had not entirely abandoned their taste for luxury, served as a fashionable hub for traders, missionaries, and military men in that region. It was there that Eliza first met Rev. Porter. Had it been a few years earlier, one could imagine the Menominee trader Queen Marinette she would have met as well.

Within one year, Eliza's tutelage of the Stuart children had grown into a de facto mission school for dozens of children. Eliza inspired such confidence and right-mindedness in the Stuarts that all children, no matter what race or how poor, were welcome to join their children in study. Meanwhile, Eliza suffered from neuralgia, a disease of the nervous system, which a doctor attempted to cure by pulling her few remaining teeth. She did not complain, instead finding humor in her hard luck. What gave her cause for complaint was the need for more missionaries. A mission school was wanted in Sault St. Marie, but there were no teachers to staff it. In her journal she wrote, "Why does the church sit in her ceiled house and this desert lie waste for lack of laborers?"

That fall, Eliza chose action over complaint. She returned to New York to recruit young women teachers and raise funds for missions. She founded the Chappell Infant School Society in Utica, an organization that enabled several missionary teachers to enter the field. In the spring she returned to Mackinaw. Freed by the arrival of additional teachers, she formed a new school on nearby St. Ignace Island. At the end of the summer another teacher had arrived to take her place there, and she moved on to Chicago. "Brother Porter" was one of the first to greet her upon her arrival.

Eliza and Jeremiah's life together began somewhat tenuously. In 1835, Rev. Porter was called to a post in Peoria and then moved to Farmington, Illinois, where the prairie stretched for miles around in a dispiriting expanse. At age twenty-eight, Eliza bore her first child, William, who died several months later. Then Jeremiah fell ill and nearly died before he recovered. Other New England pilgrims to this region lost their lives: seven ministers' wives and even more children. The illness was ascribed to the malarial climate of southern Illinois. Yet the "invalid" wife of Rev. Porter persisted in her path, bearing two more sons and helping her husband in his ministry.

When their third call came to minister at a church in Green Bay, Wisconsin, the Porters were ready to accept. After seven weeks of laborious travel and the loss of their youngest son to disease, they arrived in the "bracing" northern climate, to a region of forests and lakes, and even some familiar acquaintances. Here they lived from 1840 to 1858, raising a steadily growing family. Eliza was forty-four when she gave birth to her ninth and last child, a healthy boy. By then, few were skeptical of her hardiness.

The Porter house was a rambling cottage across from the church, with vegetable gardens, outbuildings, and a large grassy courtyard where neighborhood children came to play. Eliza would sit with her mending by the window overlooking the yard in benign supervision. In her daughter Mary's words:

> Reproofs were infrequent, bright kindly suggestions came often to the screaming, laughing company. Gallantry to girls was the fashion on that playground: was it because the soft-voiced hostess spoke so courteously to boys that she at once made them feel themselves gentlemen? There were times when the voice was not soft; that was when something cruel was done, an insect tortured, or a shrinking child teased.

. . . To many other things she was apparently deaf;
while play was good-humored and language clean, the
neighborhood were welcome to her lawn.

The household included assistant teachers, a cook, and
numerous guests, from cousins to traveling ministers and distant
parishioners. When her youngest child reached school age, Eliza
formally established an elementary school on the premises, to
which all were welcome. As her own children grew older, they were
sent to boarding school.

In the 1850s Green Bay saw the influx of peasants from
northern Europe, many of whom lived in a tenement house near
the church. Though their manners and English were coarse, Eliza
challenged her children to welcome them into their games and
study. As Mary wrote, "Our clannish unwillingness to share our
pleasures with 'Those children' was made to appear very unlovely
in our eyes, and we vied with one another in efforts to win our
bashful neighbors."

Eliza had a gift for easing the shame that recipients of charity often feel. As the wife of a frontier minister, she was in charge
of distributing occasional shipments of discarded clothing from
the East. With the children as her audience, she sorted the lot, smil-
ing mischievously when she encountered an inappropriate article,
then dispatching one of them to pack the uselessly fancy dress or
soiled item into the "far corner" of the attic. Likewise, she would
exult over items that were "just the thing" for this or that needy
parishioner. Only offerings that "relieved the need without wound-
ing the spirit of the recipient" were shared.

Rev. and Mrs. Porter were at the center of one oft-retold
episode of the Underground Railroad. The Fugitive Slave Act of
1850 created an ongoing crisis for escaped slaves living in the
North. Bounties were placed on their capture, and posses made up

of local people as well as slave owners hunted them down; if they were caught, they could be dragged back into slavery. Most of the African Americans who arrived in Wisconsin in the 1850s continued on to Canada, the only safe haven available to them.

One day the Porters received a letter from the Stockbridge Indian settlement nearby. The Mohican Indians there were sheltering a family of runaway slaves, but the correspondent feared they had been discovered. Could the Porters receive the family in Green Bay and send them out on the next steamboat to Canada?

The family—a man and his three cold hungry children—arrived at the Porters' house in the middle of the night. Every bed was already occupied; furthermore, a house full of children, no matter how well-behaved, could hardly be trusted with secrets. "Where can we hide them?" Mr. Porter asked, thinking first of the outbuildings.

As on all important matters, Eliza consulted God; according to her daughter's account, a fragment of scripture came to her mind suggesting the answer. "Perhaps the church?"

Mr. Porter responded spontaneously, "The belfry!" and there the refugees were taken, after receiving a warm, hearty meal and a change of clothes. They stayed in the bell tower for four days. As Sabbath church services approached, Eliza fretted over all the possible and even outrageous ways the family's presence might be revealed to a congregation that was not unanimously abolitionist. Just in time, the steamboat arrived in the harbor, and the family was taken to it by sailboat.

Finally, in 1858, with the clamoring courtyard emptied of all but the youngest child and his friends, the Porters decided to change their setting and left the church in Green Bay for one in Chicago. Though the family reunited there, tragedy found them: Two more of the children passed away. In her anguish, Eliza threw herself into parish work.

The nation was also undergoing painful change, and when the Civil War broke out and sons and nephews enlisted, Eliza and her husband also joined the frontline efforts, he as a chaplain, she as a field agent of the Northwest Sanitary Commission. This organization provided food, clothing, and other items to military hospitals and encampments; Eliza, in her fifties, was among the first women to join and the last to quit its service. She and her husband lived in primitive barracks, still moved by their faith to brave discomfort, risk their lives, and witness the stench of death and the groans of suffering in order to share words of reassurance and the tender gestures of parental love with the wounded, sick, and dying.

Perhaps Eliza's greatest joy in these wartime years was to participate in the founding of a school at Shiloh, Tennessee, a community of former slaves freed by the 1863 Emancipation Proclamation. In addition Eliza worked with Illinois authorities to promote the efforts of Cordelia A. P. Harvey, a colleague in the U.S. Sanitary Commission and a fellow Wisconsinite, to create military hospitals in the more healthful northern climes.

After the war Jeremiah received a new pastoral assignment. He and Eliza moved from one of the northernmost parts of the country to one of the southernmost—Brownsville, Texas. Again, Eliza began recruiting teachers and founded a school for the poor. The couple took a long trip through Mexico to familiarize themselves with the needs there. When Rev. Porter was reassigned to an Austin church, Eliza again sought out the town's least fortunate to serve.

Martha Adams, a former member of the Green Bay household who had turned to missionary work, helped in Eliza's Austin missions. Together they formed a Sunday school for freed slave children in the back room of an old stone building. She recalled Eliza engaging the young people:

She would have a multitude of little black children packed as close as their little wriggling bodies would permit. I seem to see her standing before them in that rude room upon that rough floor, her beautiful eyes beaming, her whole face illumined with love while every eye was fastened upon her face as she taught them of God and His law, of Jesus and His love.

Eliza also started a kindergarten for black children in Masontown, a settlement of former slaves in East Austin. According to Adams, the school quickly became overcrowded, and there was much discussion of how to expand it. "At length, Mrs. Porter with her characteristic faith and energy exclaimed, 'Why not devise liberal things? Why not arise and build?' The effect was electrical." The necessary money was raised, and the new school was built.

Through the lens of the present, the combination of liberal social values and conservative Biblical faith may seem paradoxical. But there was no contradiction in Eliza. As a young woman she was swept up in the religious movement of her times, adopting its slogan of salvation by faith alone. Her faith neither straightened into dogma nor rested in self-assurance; rather, she embodied it through her passionate commitment to action. In that sense, she anticipated the Social Gospel of the turn of the century: a religious movement emphasizing Christianity's ethical obligations to society and particularly to society's downtrodden.

Eliza and Jeremiah celebrated their fiftieth wedding anniversary in 1885. At a family Christmas gathering in 1887, Eliza was particularly moved by the gift of a leather photo case containing pictures of all of her children, including the departed ones. That afternoon, after meditating on some scriptures about "rest," she took a nap. In the evening she caught a chill, from which she never recovered, dying only a few days into the new year. In the weeks and months that followed, Rev. Porter was flooded with condolence letters from all parts of the country. Each narrated how Eliza had strengthened the writer's faith—how she had, through her actions, shown him or her a vision of Christ.

CORDELIA A. P. HARVEY

1824–1895

"Fresh Air" for Union Soldiers

*W*ell?" said President Lincoln upon the widow Cordelia Harvey's arrival.

It was the third time in twenty-four hours that Cordelia had seen him. She thought that she had made it fairly clear what she sought: a hospital in the north at which Union soldiers from her home state could convalesce—a hospital far removed from the swampy miasma of the southern front. It was up to the president to decide.

She was becoming familiar with President Lincoln and his curious moods. So, rather than restate her case, she simply echoed, "Well."

"Have you nothing to say?" Lincoln asked.

"Nothing, Mr. President, until I hear your decision. You bade me to come this morning; have you decided?"

"No, but I believe this idea of northern hospitals is a great humbug, and I am tired of hearing about it."

Cordelia spoke from her heart. "I regret to add a feather's weight to your already overwhelming care and responsibility. I would rather have stayed at home."

Cordelia A. P. Harvey

A gentle smile crossed the president's countenance. "I wish you had." None of his top military officials had spoken in favor of her idea. They feared that men sent north to recover would desert the cause.

"Nothing would have given me greater pleasure; but a keen sense of duty . . . made me come. The people cannot understand why their friends are left to die when with proper care they might live and do good service to their country. Mr. Lincoln, I believe you will be grateful for my coming."

She proceeded to paint, once again, the pictures she had seen—the wounded and the sick in temporary military hospitals, dying from poor ventilation. She concluded with an account of her own experience: "I know because when I was sick among them last spring, surrounded by every comfort, with the best of care, and determined to get well, I grew weaker day by day, until my friends brought me north. I recovered entirely, simply by breathing northern air."

"You assume to know more than I do," said Lincoln, abruptly.

Holding back tears, Cordelia composed herself and said, "You must pardon me, Mr. President. I intend no disrespect, but it is because of this knowledge, because I know what you do not know, that I come to you. . . . "

"You assume to know more than surgeons do."

"Oh, no!" she insisted. "But this is true—I do not come here for your favor, I am not an aspirant for military honor. . . . Now the medical authorities know as well as I do that you are opposed to establishing northern military hospitals, and they report to please you; they desire your favor. I come to you from no casual tour of inspection."

She went on to describe the cursory reviews made by the officials who inspected the hospitals, contrasting her own experience tending daily to Wisconsin men in hospitals and camps along the Mississippi River.

The mood had changed. Lincoln's brow was furrowed. "How many men does Wisconsin have in the field?" Lincoln asked. "That is, how many did your state send?"

"About 50,000 I think. I do not know exactly."

"That means there are about 20,000 now."

There was no indication where this discussion was going.

Lincoln exploded with impatience. "I have a good mind to dismiss every man of them from the service and have no more trouble with them!" It was as if an electrical impulse had passed through his body and left him pale and vulnerable.

At once surprised and sympathetic, Cordelia spoke softly of the loyalty of Wisconsin's soldiers, their desire to live and fight for their country, and if necessary, die.

Lincoln bowed his head and confessed, "I never shall be glad any more."

It was the spring of 1863, and the end of the Civil War was nowhere in sight.

After inquiring after his health, Cordelia rose and gently asked if he had made a decision on the hospitals.

"No. Come tomorrow at twelve o'clock."

✳ ✳ ✳

Cordelia Adelaide Perrine was born in Lyons, New York, in December 1824, the first of six daughters of John and Mary Perrine. Nothing is known of her early life. The Perrines were among thousands of families from upstate New York and Connecticut who migrated to Wisconsin in the 1830s and 1840s. Beginning their journey westward on the Erie Canal, such families would arrive at Buffalo, cross Lake Erie by boat, then travel overland across Michigan to destinations along Lake Michigan.

In 1842 the Perrine brood arrived in Clinton, Wisconsin, about

50 miles inland from Lake Michigan. Clinton had its first town meeting the same year; it probably numbered a few dozen farming families. Cordelia was seventeen. In the previous year a poor bookbinder and schoolteacher from Connecticut named Louis Harvey had arrived at Kenosha, on Lake Michigan. After teaching and editing the newspaper there, he was appointed postmaster and in 1847 moved to Clinton in that capacity. The courtship that led to the marriage that same year of Cordelia, age twenty-two, and Louis, age twenty-seven, is obscured by time.

The newlyweds moved to a tract of land near Clinton, in "Waterloo" (unofficially named after a band of local women who drove out their drunken husbands). Harvey bought and tore down the local distillery, built a four-story flour mill in its place, and had the town named Shopiere (French for "limestone") to replace its "spirited" past with a somewhat more sober image. In 1847 he participated in Wisconsin's constitutional convention as a member of the new Republican Party. After terms in the state senate and cabinet, Louis Harvey was elected Wisconsin's seventh governor in 1861 and took office the following January.

Louis and Cordelia's celebrations were muted by the national crisis. The Civil War had begun with the firing on Fort Sumter in the spring of 1861. When Harvey took office early in 1862, about half of Wisconsin's units had already been mustered. On April 6 at the Battle of Shiloh, Wisconsin's companies experienced their first major casualties. Deeply moved, Governor Harvey decided personally to lead an immediate relief expedition of supplies and medical staff to Tennessee. Two weeks after his departure, Cordelia was walking downtown to raise money for a family in need when she noticed the capitol and courthouse flags flying at half-mast. Panic seized her. Before anyone could tell her the news, she had read it on the faces surrounding her: Louis, her husband, was dead.

As the shock dissipated in the days and weeks that followed, the story of her husband's last days became known. First, there were the details of his senseless death: On a rainy night, transferring from one steamboat to another as he began his trip homeward, he had lost his footing and been swept down the Tennessee River. Then, there emerged a clearer picture of his mission. Those who had been with him described how tenderly and faithfully he had visited the wounded and sick Wisconsin soldiers and the joy he had brought them. A letter from Louis dated the day before his death testified: "Thank God for the impulse that brought me here. I am well and have done more good by coming than I can tell you."

These words burned in Cordelia during her months of mourning at Shopiere. By September she could no longer bear to be idle, and encouraged the notion of her appointment as Wisconsin's agent to the Western Sanitary Commission at St. Louis. Her job would be to help provide for the care of Wisconsin's wounded there, much as her husband had done in his final days, and to report back to the new governor. Thus, it was arranged. After visiting the hospital in St. Louis as charged, she embarked almost immediately to Cape Girardeau, some 120 miles south on the Mississippi River, to tend to the reputedly large numbers of sick in the military hospital there.

Though not as dramatic as shouldering a musket, Cordelia's role was every bit as important. In the Civil War diseases like typhoid and pneumonia, not to mention chronic diarrhea, constituted a greater threat than enemy fire. Deaths from these and other diseases outnumbered those from battle injuries by roughly two to one. In Wisconsin's First Infantry Cavalry, the group then stationed at Cape Girardeau, the ratio of those dying from disease was much worse. While 67 were killed on the battlefield, 321 were lost to disease.

Cordelia was appalled by the dirty, crowded conditions in the Cape Girardeau hospital, a former school building with poor ventilation. The men she met looked like ghosts, and crowded around her begging for release from duty and expressing their wish to join her husband in death. She witnessed several deaths and deemed the surgeon incompetent. Her opinion of the officers of the regiment was no higher. Cordelia held nothing back in her first letter to the governor: "When the history of this regiment is known the English language will fail to express the indignation of the people over the destruction of some of the noblest men that ever our state sent into the service. Not destroyed for their Countries [*sic*] good but sacrificed to the caprices, whims & wickedness of a Madman." The reference to the "madman," like much else in the letter, was clouded by passion, although her next letter revealed the reference to be to Colonel Edward Daniels, who led unauthorized raids in Arkansas and was dismissed later that year. The only request she made was for "one or two good surgeons."

Her second letter suggests a professionalism missing in her first. It began with a sober explanation of her actions: "Though not strictly in the line of my instructions, I felt it my duty to repair to Cape Girardeau," adding that the Wisconsin men in the St. Louis hospital were sufficiently cared for. She listed the supplies she obtained from the warehouse in St. Louis: 150 bosom shirts, 100 hospital shirts, 100 pillow slips, and so on. In addition to clean clothes and linens, soap, and sponges, she had requested and been promised two bottles of sherry, three of port, ten jars of jelly, and so on. Cordelia quickly perceived that small servings of such treats were vital to the spirits of the troops.

Interestingly enough, the letter was written from Madison. Cordelia had realized that the generosity of the commission depended on the generosity of civilians, and she was determined not to let that falter. She spent the next day composing a letter to the *Wisconsin Daily State Journal* appealing to the women of her state to send their care packages not to the regiments but to the warehouse in St. Louis, whence they would be distributed with a professional efficiency. "The Sanitary Commission is now a system from which flow untold comforts to the sick and suffering. Let us see to it that the channels which replenish this fountain be made wide and deep, and kept full of every good." She went on to list the needed items: clothing, blankets, dried fruit, and cooking supplies such as tapioca and arrowroot. And of course, wines and jellies.

Early in her service, Cordelia had discovered another in-humanity of the system: its unwillingness to discharge or furlough fatally ill soldiers. Certificates of disability signed by the doctor invariably came back from higher-ups in St. Louis "disapproved."

Perhaps it took a woman to overcome the system's failure. In a lecture after the war, Cordelia described how one mother of a gravely sick soldier had actually traveled to St. Louis, desperately trying to bring him back home to Wisconsin. In tears, she told Cordelia her story, showing her the certificate, signed first by the doctor and then by the medical director, "disapproved." Cordelia took the certificate and went immediately to the medical director's office.

"What do you want?" he asked.

"To talk with you a moment, General," she replied.

"No time for talking."

"I will wait."

Cordelia did not budge as the general pretended to go about his business. Finally, he asked what she wanted. She told the woman's story, asking the general in St. Louis to imagine that it was his son languishing at the Soldier's Home. He asked her to imag-ine the reprimand he would receive for disobeying regulations.

"They will rap me over the knuckles at Washington."

"Oh, that your knuckles were mine. I would be willing to have them skinned; the skin would grow back, you know."

"Suppose I do approve these papers, it will do no good. The general in command will stop them and censure me."

"But you will have done all you could and have obeyed the higher law."

This rhetoric convinced him, and he never disputed another case she brought to his attention.

Cordelia herself struggled between "higher" and "lower" laws when she reached the hospital in Memphis, housing 1,500 inmates. Her job was to tend to the Wisconsin ill, but there were many more needing her attention. She was asked to compile a list of all the men who deserved furlough—cripples, consumptives, feeble men, and boys—and thus visited every single one of them to determine for herself his chances of recovery. By the end of this monumental task, she had not only freed hundreds of men from suffering but had earned the respect of the surgeons and military men. It was for actions like this that she was publicly dubbed "The Nightingale of Wisconsin" and "The Angel from Wisconsin," epithets she disavowed. ("I do not wish to be 'Florence Nightengaled' nor any thing of the kind.") In the end her dutiful service to all the Union soldiers only enhanced her powers to advocate for Wisconsin's suffering men. On one occasion a soldier had lain five months with typhoid fever. Cordelia not only arranged his discharge, but also managed to finance his trip home by demanding he be paid for the time he had spent in the hospital.

Almost every one of Cordelia's letters to the governor reviles the crowded, contagious air or "miasma" of hospital facilities. She saw her role as metaphorically "airing out" the places she visited. Her role was to "refresh" the men with a drop of wine or an attentive ear, in her own words, "always taking with her from the outside world fresh air, fresh flowers, and all the hope and comfort she could find in her heart to give them." In a man's world, her undaunted style made her indeed a "breath of fresh air." It was this originality and verve that attracted President Lincoln to her, a woman of 38 known to be more "handsome" than "appealing."

Nonetheless, as she described to President Lincoln, she, too, fell ill from the miasma, and retreated to Madison for a quick cure.

By then fully understanding the inertia of the "regular channels" of masculine authority, she decided to plead her case for northern hospitals to the commander-in-chief in person.

On her fourth visit to Lincoln that week in April 1863, Cordelia finally received his verdict on her request. Lincoln informed her that "an order equivalent to granting a hospital in your state has been issued nearly twenty-four hours." In other words, he had made his decision almost immediately after their last interview.

Cordelia was nearly speechless. "God bless you. I thank you in the name of thousands who will bless you for the act." Then, realizing the mountain of opposition she had moved, she asked, "Do you mean, really and truly, that we are going to have a hospital now?"

He looked at her and said, "I do most certainly hope so."

Cordelia arrived the following morning, as instructed, for a copy of the order and for her last visit with Lincoln. When she arrived at the White House, the waiting room was full. She was summoned in immediately.

The President asked her to sit. Handing her the order, he said, "I suppose you would have been mad if I had said no."

She replied, "I should not have been angry, Mr. Lincoln. I should only have arrived earlier this morning than I did."

"I think I acted wisely, then," Lincoln said with a laugh, then added, "Don't you ever get angry?"

Cordelia responded, "I never get angry when I have an object to gain; to get angry, you know, would only weaken my cause, and destroy my influence."

Clearly impressed with the might of this widow, Lincoln asked to name the hospital after her. Cordelia demurred. Begging his forgiveness, she expressed her wish to have it named for her late husband, the governor. Lincoln said some appreciative words about him and wrote a message for her to the Secretary of War and gave it to her to take to him.

She thanked him. "You have been very kind to me and I am grateful for it."

According to her account, Lincoln looked up at her from under his thick eyebrows and said, "You almost think me handsome, don't you?"

His face was so lit with benevolence and kindness that she responded impulsively. "You are perfectly lovely to me, now, Mr. Lincoln," at which he blushed and then laughed "most heartily." As he clasped her hand in his own, a hand "in which there was so much power and so little beauty," she bent to kiss it "as I would my country's shrine," then left with his good-bye.

Thus was Harvey Hospital established in Madison, Wisconsin, along with two other Union hospitals in the state. Two months later thousands of those wounded at Gettysburg would be sent by rail to northern hospitals for treatment. Cordelia's mission was an idea whose time had come.

Cordelia returned to her duties, no less zealous in their discharge for the remarkable drama in which she had acted so bravely. The year 1864 found her reporting from the Deep South to the new Wisconsin governor. He, too, had to be "broken in." "I should at once comply with your wish for me to go to Memphis did I not feel that I was much more needed here," she wrote from New Orleans. In the same letter, she asked for the state to charter a boat to bring the wounded north, to avoid the summer heat.

It was from a Sanitary Commission hospital boat that she expressed herself most vividly about the cause of the war, as well as its horrors. In the hold below were hundreds of former slaves of all descriptions, "from babies a few months old to old gray haired men & women." After describing how she doled out canned peaches on crackers to the wounded soldiers above ("Oh that the one that sent them could have seen the grateful, tearful eyes of the sons, brothers, fathers and husbands as I saw them that day"), she turned to the war's most recent horror. Fort Pillow, near Memphis, manned by equal numbers of freed slaves and Tennessee Union soldiers, had been forced to surrender to a Confederate force that greatly outnumbered them. In the action that followed, more than 200 African-American soldiers were massacred.

Cordelia described the Fort Pillow fallout with a respectful awe. "Our officers of negro regiments declare they will take no more prisoners—& there is death to the rebel in every black man's eye. They are still but terrible. *They will fight*." To illustrate the almost spiritual power she saw in these fighters, she told of a man who had one arm shot off and the other shattered by gunfire, yet who was "*alive!* with other life than his own! When told that it was doubtful if he lived, he said bless the Lord I have done my duty fighting for my country & my brethren & I die a man, & a *free* man." She added that he, in fact, survived amputation well, then concluded her letter with a note of grim alliance: "The negroes know what they are doing."

One year later, and one week after Lee's surrender, Cordelia wrote from Vicksburg about the conclusion of the war. "I have all the goods that I can distribute," and she had heard all the stories she could bear to hear. "Volumes could be filled with thrilling incidents, but I have not heart to report them, or time to write them."

After the war Cordelia petitioned the state to convert Harvey Hospital into an orphanage for soldiers' children. Appealing to the great sacrifice Wisconsin's soldiers had made, she won over to her idea prominent financial and political leaders, who in turn pushed the issue through the state legislature. The Soldiers' Orphans' Home became a state responsibility. Cordelia herself served as its superintendent for the first year. It lasted a decade in downtown Madison, providing significantly better care than most orphanages of the day. By the time it closed, most Civil War orphans were old enough to care for themselves.

In 1876 Cordelia Harvey married the Reverend Albert Chester and moved to Buffalo, New York, where she taught school. She returned to Wisconsin after his death.

Cordelia died in 1895 and was buried in Madison's Forest Hill Cemetery next to her husband, the governor. She liked to close her letters with the modest assertion that "some good" had been accomplished through her service. To which, across the centuries, we must reply, "Much was."

MARGARETHE MEYER SCHURZ
1833–1876

Envoy of the Kindergarten

*I*n the fall of 1859, Margarethe Meyer Schurz, once an heiress from Hamburg, then a prominent woman of Watertown, Wisconsin, accompanied her husband, the radical politician Carl Schurz, to the East Coast, where he would spend the season lecturing. She stayed at the home of some friends in Philadelphia, the city where she and Carl had spent their first three years in America, and made occasional excursions to visit other eastern friends she had made during that period. While visiting one friend in Boston, she happened to meet Elizabeth Peabody, who wrote of the occasion as one of the turning points in America's educational history.

At fifty-five, Elizabeth Peabody was a highly respected intellectual among the New England Transcendentalists, an independent publisher and writer whose combined library–bookstore in downtown Boston was frequented by friends such as Ralph Waldo Emerson, Henry David Thoreau, Margaret Fuller, Nathaniel Hawthorne, and the educator Horace Mann. In fact the latter two were married to her two younger sisters. Elizabeth herself had

MRS. CARL SCHURZ
First kindergarten teacher in the United States.
Conducted such a School at Watertown in 1857.

Margarethe Meyer Schurz

never married. Among her many lifelong intellectual interests—she spoke nearly a dozen languages—were the educational theories and models emerging in Europe at the time.

Twenty-six-year-old Margarethe was reasonably accomplished at music and languages—she spoke two. She had two small children in tow and was not yet altogether at home in her adoptive country.

Evidently the four children of the Boston friend were badly misbehaving before Margarethe joined the get-together where she would meet Elizabeth. Their father, according to Elizabeth, "had a theory that children should only be dealt with as irresponsible beings before they were six years old, at which age he proposed to put on the screws of discipline." Into this mayhem walked Margarethe with her daughters Agathe, age six, and Marianna, four. As the two families of children merged and commenced their play, Agathe's alert and self-possessed influence caught Elizabeth's attention—it was like "a calm coming upon the storm of young life."

Elizabeth commented to Margarethe, "That child of yours is a miracle, so childlike and unconscious, and yet so wise and able, attracting and ruling the children, who seem nothing short of enchanted."

Margarethe responded, "No miracle, but only brought up in a kindergarten."

One can imagine that she pronounced the German term proudly. Based on the German words for *child* and *garden*, the expression had been coined by the educational theorist Friedrich Froebel in 1840. While just a teenager in Hamburg, Margarethe had attended Froebel's fashionable lecture course, then helped her sister establish the first kindergarten in England. While the concept had caused quite a stir in Germany, enough to prompt the Prussian government to close all kindergartens and denounce their proponents as atheists, in America the kindergarten and its inventor were still unknown, except to a lucky few in Watertown, Wisconsin.

When asked, Margerethe explained that a kindergarten is "a garden whose plants are humans." She described its principle of organized play and compared it to the methods of Pestalozzi, the Italian educational reformer whose work was better known in the United States. Finally, she offered to send her new friend a section of Froebel's handbook, *The Education of Mankind*.

According to Elizabeth, "Out of this pamphlet, together with this conversation and the glimpse of the perfect growth of a child grew the first practical attempt at a kindergarten in Boston." The next year Elizabeth began the first English-speaking kindergarten in the United States. She went on to lead the kindergarten movement in the United States, founding the journal the *Kindergarten Messenger* and training scores of kindergarten teachers.

Margarethe's contributions were not so far ranging. She only lived into her forties, suffering from a number of complaints, ranging from a persistent cough and more serious lung ailments to homesickness for Germany and frustration with her husband's frequent absences. Her unique story, though, has its own fascination, especially as it weaves its way through the German chapters of Wisconsin history.

* * *

Before Froebel, educators had written for men as their "natural" intellectual counterparts. By contrast Froebel spoke and wrote directly to women, promoting early childhood education as an extension of mothering. This makes the circumstances of Margarethe Meyer's birth particularly noteworthy: Her mother died in childbirth, leaving her to be raised by an aunt. When her father died ten years later, her older brothers assumed responsibility for her. One can only speculate how those events affected her, but it is easy to imagine that her desire to practice an enlightened motherhood was fueled by her own experience of childhood. She must have wanted to give her children the best of what had been missing from her own life.

Margarethe's father and older brothers were wealthy sugarcane merchants in Hamburg, a historic trading center located near the mouth on the Elbe River on the North Sea. Broad-minded and progressive, they were friends with a large group of scientists, writers, and musicians: In short, they were members of the educated business class known as the bourgeoisie. This group was discontented with the government in Germany at the time. Indeed, there was no Germany. Large portions were ruled by the King of Prussia; others were small, independent states. This fragmentation was bad for business and bad for groups who traditionally faced discrimination, such as Jews and peasants. Even though Hamburg was a free city, Margarethe would have been surrounded by hopes for a single Germany united under a constitution.

In 1848 liberals at universities throughout Germany attempted a revolution to achieve this dream of unification. (Countries in similar situations, like Italy, attempted similar revolutions at the same time.) One leader of the movement was a German professor at the University of Bonn named Gottfried Kinkel. When Kinkel was captured and imprisoned, young Carl Schurz, a student at Bonn, gained national fame—and exile status—by dramatically rescuing his teacher and spiriting him off to England. The 1848 revolution was unsuccessful, and the resulting harsh crackdown caused many Germans to flee to England. Still more fled to America, where the form of government they sought for Germany already existed.

Meanwhile, in Hamburg, Margarethe's sister Berthe had

formed a group with a Jewish author to promote friendship between Christian and Jewish women. The mission of the group evolved, and in 1850 it invited Froebel to Hamburg to train mothers and kindergarten teachers in his methods.

The Froebelian system of teaching began with simple, cheerful songs; it then moved to object lessons featuring balls and cubes. On the surface this might sound like an ordinary kindergarten, but its buoyant motto—"Come, let us live with our children!"—was revolutionary to a culture that saw children as defective adults and did not spare the rod of discipline. However, unlike modern educational practice, Froebel's work had a strong spiritual dimension. Here he is, for instance, explaining the "deep significance" of balls as playthings: "The child, feeling himself a whole, early seeks and must seek in conformity with his human nature and his destiny, even at the stage of unconsciousness, always to contemplate, to grasp, and to possess a whole." The mother-teacher is supposed to be conscious of these lofty ideas as she handles the ball with the child.

Sixteen-year-old Margarethe attended these lectures with her sister Berthe, and evidently took the best notes of all those who were there, for when Froebel saw them, he declared them better than all of his books and asked if he could edit them for publication. Unfortunately, though, this manuscript was lost in the mail en route to the publisher and was never found.

In a rapid sequence of events, Berthe fell in love with a defrocked priest, divorced her husband to marry him, moved with him to London, and began the first Froebelian kindergarten to be established outside of Germany. Soon after she became pregnant, and Margarethe joined the household to help with the kindergarten. Here was a chance for Margarethe to put to use the theory she had learned—not to mention her lovely singing voice.

Then, late in 1851, Carl Schurz visited Berthe's husband. Here is Carl's description of the event:

> My business was soon disposed of and I rose to go, when he opened the door and called out into an adjacent room, "Margarethe, come in if you please, here is a gentleman whom you would probably like to know." A girl of about 18 entered; of stately stature, a dark, curly head, something childlike in her beautiful features, and large, dark, truthful eyes. . . . [The meeting] did not pass over without some embarrassment. On her part, because she had in her fancy attributed to me all sorts of great qualities, and therefore been a little afraid of me. On my part, because I had not quite overcome my youthful bashfulness in the presence of women. Our first conversation touched only such ordinary things as common acquaintances, and we parted with the expression of hope that we might meet again. We did indeed meet again; not very soon, but then very often, and [in] not less than a year, I was to be joined to this girl for life.

The story of their engagement is particularly charming. Evidently the two walked about London all that day, telling their life stories to each other. It was raining, and by the end of the day, the green dye from Margarethe's hat had stained her face and clothes. So enchanted had they been with each other, they had neither noticed nor cared! That evening they decided to marry. Of course Carl had first to convince Margarethe's brothers that he, a penniless refugee, could properly care for their sister.

Carl Schurz's letters to Adolph Meyer show how passionate he was about Margarethe and how optimistic he was for their future in America. It was the one place where being a citizen could hold meaning for him. Furthermore, it would be good for Margarethe, who, he recognized, had not yet found "true content." According to Schurz, this was simply because her life thus far had been too easy: "Problems had been lacking in her life." Margarethe's "physical and mental health" depended on the stimulation a more demanding situation could provide. While Carl thus alluded to Margarethe's ill health, he was no more able than later historians to define it as strictly physical or mental. It seemed to be a combination. Of course, as young lovers will do, he discounted his partner's weakness, believing he knew its remedy: work!

Margarethe's substantial inheritance enabled the newlyweds to travel first-class on their trans-Atlantic voyage, sustained their association with the wealthiest families in Philadelphia, and financed several recuperative trips back and forth to Germany. Her money also helped with the birth of their first child, Agathe. Her fortune was finally exhausted, however, by Carl's eventual down payment on property located in Watertown, Wisconsin. With a population of 10,000, Watertown was in the 1850s the second largest city in Wisconsin. It expected railroad connections to Milwaukee and Chicago and a large German population, including some of Carl's relatives. It was because of these relations that Wisconsin had always been Carl's planned destination. Unfortunately, the town would shrink in relative importance as the years progressed, voiding most of the financial advantage with which the Schurzes had begun their American life. Carl's developing talent as a speaker and politician would soon become the family's primary financial asset.

Carl's parents and sisters had arrived in America in 1854, and he convinced them to settle in Watertown, finding them a house in town. Within a year, his sisters were married and running a millinery shop, with children on the way. But Margarethe did not want to go west. Philadelphia wasn't Hamburg, but it was better than living on the frontier!—so she thought. In fact Wisconsin was developing rapidly at the time. Letters from Carl written while he was scouting for property in Watertown play up the town's cultural goings-on: a German singing group, amateur theater, and numerous balls on one trip, an operatic group on the next. Twice Margarethe fell ill; twice she and Carl went to Europe to "recover"; their second child, Marianna, was born overseas.

Finally, in 1855, Carl exerted his authority and purchased a farm atop a hill outside of Watertown. Writing to Margarethe, he described it in glowing terms: "We are all quite enraptured by the place. . . . On the left the stream, shining out between tall trees; directly in front of me, the town with its friendly white houses; beyond and to my right, wooded hills and a luscious strip of green meadow land." Margarethe capitulated, and moved.

The house, once completed, was spacious and elegant, with a bay window in the room where Margarethe enjoyed sitting, a study for Carl with a bright red carpet, and a piano, on which Margarethe could play. Once settled, Margarethe appears to have enjoyed life in Waterown. She joined the local singing society and welcomed a steady stream of guests to their home. Carl's *Reminiscences* tells of the parties held there, including one costume ball that lasted into the morning when a heavy snowfall made it impossible for guests to leave.

And, of course, there was the kindergarten. It began with an invitation to Agathe and Marianna's four little cousins, daughters of Carl's sisters, to play and sing with them. A neighbor girl came to teach the girls English and care for Marianna. Then Margarethe launched into the full Froebelian system, including gift boxes containing a ball for each child, and singing beside the piano. She moved the location of the school to the Schurz family house in town, to make it more convenient for other children to come. At twenty-four years of age, she had unwittingly made history in America.

Meanwhile, Carl was making history in his own way. Most Germans were Democrats, the party of working-class immigrants. Carl had joined the new Republican Party because of its stance against slavery. He knew other Germans shared his values; they only needed some encouragement to switch parties. And there was no one better than the hero of 1848 to do the encouraging. Carl ran for local offices with the help of Cordelia A. P. Harvey's husband, Louis, then went out of state to mobilize the German vote for Lincoln in the 1858 Illinois senate race—the campaign of the famous Lincoln–Douglas debates. Carl campaigned for Lincoln again in 1860, securing the great man's friendship and respect. The German vote in the Midwestern states is believed by many historians to have been the key to Lincoln's victory.

During these years Lincoln met Margarethe on several occasions. Carl had held out for a European appointment from the new president, largely for Margarethe's sake, and was finally appointed ambassador to Spain. When the outbreak of the Civil War inspired Carl to request to serve his country in a military role instead, Lincoln, with his teasing humor, asked, "Have you talked the matter over with that handsome, dear wife of yours?"

"Yes," Carl said, "She thought it was pretty hard, but she is a good patriot."

"If she agrees," said Lincoln, "then I do."

From her letters this depiction of her patriotic attitude seems accurate. In 1862, before he began fighting, Margarethe and a woman friend undertook a two-day trip from Philadelphia to Carl's encampment in Middletown, Virginia. After six days during which she and her friend hung wreaths, helped with the cooking, and gained a sense of his popularity as brigadier general, the call to march finally came. Margarethe writes, somewhat naively, "Oh, how gladly Carl would have taken me along and how gladly I should have gone, but [Carl's commander] thought it unadvisable." She returned to her friend's farm in Philadelphia, where she stayed for the duration of the war.

In April 1865 the war ended, Lincoln was shot, and Margarethe had her third child, Emma Savannah. When Carl rejoined his wife, three daughters, and parents at Watertown several months later, it soon became clear that the family was bankrupt and faced foreclosure of the farm. Carl found newspaper jobs first in Detroit, then St. Louis, while Margarethe fell ill and went to Germany following the death of her newborn, Emma. While Carl had become the quintessential American immigrant—dynamic, self-made, and bringing extended family with him—Margarethe never gave up her ties to the Old World, where all of her family still lived. Thus, her life remained a constant shuttle between the two continents.

Margarethe was in Germany in 1869 when Carl won a seat in the U.S. Senate from Missouri. When she arrived in Washington, she followed his career there with interest, though perhaps with not as much interest and energy as her "successor," Belle Case La Follette, the wife of the legendary Wisconsin senator, Robert "Fighting Bob" La Follette. Both of these intelligent, capable women, like many women since them, were drawn to dynamic politicians, perhaps unconsciously, as their entree to the public sphere, from which they, as women, were by custom practically banned. When in Washington, Margarethe often watched the proceedings from the viewer's gallery of the Senate; when she was elsewhere, Carl remained in constant "conversation" with her concerning the details of his career, never condescending to her in his frequent and affectionate letters.

Margarethe's difficulties bring into focus the tremendous challenges facing women in earlier times, when so little was known about health care, birth control, and mental illness. She was known as a querulous woman, though all her hypochondria and home-sickness seemed not to dampen Schurz's love for her. On the one hand, she probably suffered from depression; on the other, repeated childbirth took its toll. She delivered Carl Lincoln at age thirty-eight and Herbert at age forty-three. Her death two days after Herbert's birth left the infant motherless, just as her mother's death had left her.

BELLE CASE
LA FOLLETTE
1859–1931

"Having It All, Giving Her All"

*B*elle Case La Follette sat down at the kitchen table in the governor's mansion for a few quiet moments of reflection. What a difficult summer it had been! When the state legislature disbanded in May without having enacted a single Progressive law, her husband Bob had collapsed from depression. He lay in his bed for months, while Belle handled most of his work herself.

Less than a year earlier, Robert Marion La Follette had been elected governor by a landslide vote. The public loved his reform agenda. Belle knew; she had accompanied him on his 6,433-mile "whistle stop" campaign tour. The audiences had been awakened to the promise of true democracy—government of, by, and for the *people*, not by the special interests. They wanted to have more of a voice in government, to change, for instance, election primary rules so that voters, and not party hacks, decided on their candidates. They wanted to lessen the influence of big corporations on government, to restrict the unfair perks they gave politicians. The voters had become better informed because of Bob's candidacy. To top it off, Bob had done beautifully in his address to the new senate

Belle Case La Follette

and assembly. Belle herself had deemed the speech "perfect"—not a word she used lightly.

Unfortunately for his program, Governor La Follette was the only Progressive Republican whom Wisconsin had elected in 1900. The people had elected as legislators the usual politicians, most of them so-called "Stalwart" Republicans who generally voted as demanded by the business interests who controlled the party. They were the reason why Bob's program had failed his first year.

Belle thought awhile about her husband's predicament. He had so much faith in the people—perhaps too much faith. He took for granted that the voters knew what went on in the legislative halls of Madison, when, in fact, many paid no attention or had no way to find out. How could Wisconsin voters be educated? *I'm the educator,* Belle thought. *I should be able to find a way.*

Thus was born the idea of the *Voter's Hand-Book,* a guide published by the La Follettes revealing how each Wisconsin legislator had voted on the laws Bob had proposed. At the time such a thing was unheard-of. It was for advice such as this that Bob described Belle as his "wisest and best counselor," the person whose judgment he always consulted first. During the next campaign Bob passed out the *Hand-Book* and cited it in his speeches. The strategy worked. The most corrupt of the Stalwarts were voted out of office, and Bob's reforms went forward. Years later, when he was a U.S. Senator and faced the same kind of opposition in Washington, he used the strategy again, sharing his colleagues' voting records despite their complaints that he was violating "senatorial courtesy."

Belle Case La Follette was more than an educator and more than a devoted counselor to her husband. She was a writer, a lawyer, a suffragist, and a crusader for peace. She was a horsewoman. She was even a jogger before it was in vogue to be so. In addition to all these things, Belle was a loving and intelligent mother of four children. Her desire to "have it all" was decisively modern, but in Belle's case, it also meant "giving her all." She defined her "duty" in the most broad-minded, idealistic standards possible, then set out with courage and vigor to satisfy that duty.

* * *

Belle Case started her life as a farm girl, born in a log cabin in Summit, Wisconsin, in 1859. When she was three, the family moved to Baraboo to be closer to her paternal grandparents. She adored her grandmother, Lucetta Moore Case, who spun and dyed wool and wove it into Scotch plaids for the family's clothing, kept bees for honey, made rag rugs, and told time by the stars—a model of self-sufficiency and pioneer capability. Lucetta and Belle's mother, Mary, recognized Belle's intelligence and made certain that she got educated. Though the schoolhouse was a mile away, Belle never missed a day nor was tardy, and she received excellent scores. When she expressed her wish to study at the University of Wisconsin, Mary expanded her butter-and-egg business to pay for Belle's room and board.

Belle met Bob in her first-semester German class, and the two became fast friends. They shared farm backgrounds, literary ambitions, and a passion for the social good. They collaborated on speechmaking—at the time both a required and a popular extracurricular activity: She edited his speeches, and he taught her to overcome her fear of public speaking. Belle's orations argued for more "natural" approaches to child-rearing and education, while Bob's gravitated to the theme of injustice. To further his causes, he actually purchased the semimonthly college newspaper, then had to work so hard to keep up with the paper and repay his debt that he found himself needing Belle, an "A" student, to tutor him in his courses.

Bob was infatuated with his short, sturdy, blue-eyed comrade. On the other hand, she had reservations about him. Later, he would tell the children that she laughed when he first proposed to her. He persisted, and won an engagement at the end of their junior year, but it was another year before the engagement was announced, and two more years before they were married. After graduating Belle taught high school for two years, the second in her hometown of Baraboo. Most states then had laws that female teachers could not marry, making her choice between "marriage" and "career" fairly clear-cut. When Belle and Bob finally wed on January 1, 1881, Belle vowed "to love and to honor" but not "to obey"; she specifically asked the Unitarian minister to omit that traditional promise from the ceremony.

In the meantime Bob had become a lawyer and had become district attorney of Dane County. In 1882 he opened a law practice with his sister's husband, whose Madison residence Belle and he shared. Shortly after Belle gave birth to their first child, Fola, Belle decided that she could have a career after all and enrolled in the University of Wisconsin's law school. She became the school's first female graduate in 1885, and immediately found a way to put her skills to work.

The previous fall Bob had been elected to the U.S. House of Representatives, where he would serve for three terms, through 1890. In Washington, Belle frequently watched the House debates from the balcony, particularly when Bob was to propose a bill or make a speech. In those days before large legislative office staffs, Belle acted as Bob's lone clerk, helping with much of his research and correspondence. Her thoughtful, well-written letters gave the Wisconsin voters back home a sense of connectedness. As an extra personal touch, Belle often included packets of seeds, available free from the U.S. Patent Office.

While Belle enjoyed the intellectual life of the capital, she did not relish the social life embodied by many politicians' wives—in her words, "women without any special occupation, whose thoughts were centered on society, dress, cards, and gossip." Only by using the endless ritual of "social calls" to ferret out information about each politician's legislative interests was this "duty" made bearable for her.

When his six-year service in the House ended, Bob returned to his law practice, which expanded so quickly that Belle was needed to write briefs, including one for a case that won on an appeal to the Wisconsin Supreme Court. However, Belle did not wish to engage in the private practice of law. Instead, she returned to raising children. Between 1895 and 1899, she gave birth to Robert Jr., Philip, and Mary. Luckily for Belle, Fola was older and could be counted on to help with child care. Despite Bob's political failures during this period (he ran for governor and lost in 1896 and 1898), Belle enjoyed this time in their lives. As she wrote, "Nothing was wanting to make our life complete."

One year after Mary's birth, Bob again campaigned for governor. His previous attempts, though unsuccessful, had built momentum for the Progressive cause. People had begun to understand the problems with the current system and became more receptive to his solutions. With Belle at his side, he finally won. The family of six moved into the governor's mansion on the shore of Lake Mendota, where they stayed for four years.

Belle coped with the new pressures associated with Bob's executive office by leading a simple life and maintaining the family's health. She was committed to a clean or what she called "hygenic" house, and was unafraid of housework. The farm girl in her encouraged the children's inclination toward rowdy outdoor games, and in an era of corsets and bustles, she herself donned comfortable clothes and jogged around the mansion's grounds. Needless to say, the "society women" who lived in the neighbor-

hood rarely called on her, but she and Bob did occasionally enter-
tain at the mansion: Her rule of thumb was always to seat the
interesting guests next to the dull ones.

In 1904, when Governor La Follette was elected senator by
the Wisconsin legislature, Bob bought a 60-acre farm in Madison,
to which the family could retreat from political life. Belle was reluctant to incur so much debt and knew the farm would greatly
expand her duties, but she could not resist. Between life on the
farm and in Washington, where the family rented a flat, all aspects
of the children's lives—physical, intellectual, civic, spiritual—
could be nurtured. At "Maple Bluff" they kept horses and dairy
cows, a herd of Shetland ponies, ducks and chickens, and had several kinds of fruit orchards, grapevines, and a kitchen vegetable
garden. Never complaining of the work, Belle described the farm
as a comfort and a pleasure; it made her life rich.

Belle once wrote, "The home is the foundation of society.
Government exists for society. Home, society, government are best
when men and women . . . have the widest range of common interests, the most to think about, to talk about." Elizabeth Evans, a fellow activist and soon after they met, a friend, saw this
egalitarianism played out in the relationship between the genera-
tions in the La Follette household, as well: "There was a solidarity
about the La Follette family beyond that of any other I have ever
encountered. The children took part in every discussion and
expressed their opinions freely. There was never an attempt to
impose the opinion of the grown-ups upon them. Always, they
were treated as persons." When Evans made these observations,
Robert Jr. was fifteen, Phil was thirteen, and Mary was eleven; Fola,
twenty-seven, was on tour as the star of a one-act comedy about
women's suffrage, *How the Vote Was Won*. The two boys would go on
to achieve prominence in politics, both as third party "Progres-
sives"—Robert Jr. as a three-term U.S. senator and Phil a three-

term governor of Wisconsin. All shared Belle and Bob's idealism, though they were not immune to the negative side effects of the high expectations held for them. The suicide of Robert Jr. in 1953 may have been an attempt to protect the family name from the smears of his Wisconsin rival, Senator Joseph McCarthy. It is certainly safe to say that the La Follettes defined and dominated the politics of Wisconsin for several decades and that they suffered for their notoriety.

The solidarity Evans describes is reflected in the frequent and affectionate letters between siblings and parents, as the family coped with living in two places at once. Like her contribution to her husband's groundbreaking career, the lifelong intimacy the family shared must be seen as one of Belle's proudest achievements. However, as the children grew older and Bob's role in the Senate became more secure, Belle emerged as a more independent woman. She began to develop friendships with other progressive women and carve out her own space for reform.

The beginning of this transformation occurred with Bob's decision in 1909 to start a magazine to spread the "Progressive gospel"; in fact, the magazine was later renamed *The Progressive* and continues today as a monthly publication. In its beginnings, *La Follette's Magazine*, as it was called, was a weekly publication backed solely by Bob's money and the farm property. It was a major undertaking, and Belle was at the center of it.

Belle was the women's page editor, though hers was hardly an ordinary "women's page." In her weekly column she discussed everything from capital punishment to the need for city planning and women's suffrage, along with the traditional women's subjects of children and education. She also selected letters from readers for publication and solicited reports from various reform movements led by women.

Belle flourished in this medium. She debuted by recommending physical exercise to her readers:

- We women are too much inclined to wrestle inwardly with a bad feeling. The same effort directed to putting the body in healthy action will make the spirit normal. (1909)

- There is no such good all-round exercise as running. (1909)

She then moved quickly to more controversial subjects:

- The joys of labor are as important as the joys of owning and using. (1909)

- From infancy we parents should guard against any sense of ownership of our children. We are trustees, not proprietors. (1911)

- Whatever its merits, there is something radically wrong in our system of education which, from kindergarten through the professional course, keeps the young under continuous strain without keeping them really interested from within. (1911)

- Capital punishment is a survival of barbarism and its existence is contrary to the best thought and practice of modern civilization. (1912)

- For years the federal government has spent enormous sums of money annually gathering and disseminating information about the diseases of cattle, hogs and horses, but has done nothing to prevent the great waste of child life. (1912)

The two greatest challenges to Belle as the women's editor of *La Follette's Magazine* came during Woodrow Wilson's presidency. The first was the president's tacit acceptance of attempts to segregate government offices. In the large Treasury Department, blacks and whites who had worked together for years were now required to use separate lunchroom tables. Like the "freedom fighters" who sat at the Woolworth's counters forty years later, three African-American women refused to follow the new rules. Belle supported their protest in her column, interviewed one of the women, Rosebud Murraye, and wrote letters to the treasury secretary and President Wilson forcefully criticizing the policy. She reprinted the correspondence in the women's pages of *La Follette's*, along with the hate mail she received from angry readers. The subject so moved her that she made speeches against lynching, segregation, and the denial of blacks' voting rights. She and others refused to remain silent on the issue, and in 1914, Wilson finally re-integrated government offices.

Then, in July of 1914, war broke out in Europe. Belle responded in her column, reporting on anti-war organizations and voicing her concern about the scapegoating of German Americans such as those among whom she had grown up in rural Wisconsin. As the death toll in Europe mounted, Jane Addams, the great Chicago reformer, organized the Women's Peace Party. Belle attended the first meeting along with 3,000 others. Only one newspaper reported on the event, but Belle printed the meeting's resolution in *La Follette's* in its entirety. It demanded that a convention of neutral nations be called upon to keep the war from spreading. It also demanded limits on arms manufacturing. The anti-war measures Bob proposed in the Senate were based on the Party's platform. However, whatever support existed in the country for their position was soon beaten back by political propaganda. Most notably, former president Teddy Roosevelt belittled the women as "silly and base," claiming that they had "abandon[ed their] national duty."

The sinking of the *Lusitania*, a British trading vessel with American passengers and American weapons aboard, heightened the war fever. Addams went to Europe to found the Women's International League for Peace and Freedom. Though she was unable to attend the meeting, Belle was designated a charter member. Meanwhile, President Wilson pushed for war, asking for $1.5 billion in weapons and military training, while cutting the budget of the Children's Bureau, an office that Belle had helped lobby into existence. Belle reported and commented on all of this fearlessly. She wrote that "the people who say 'stand by the President, right or wrong' " were not living up to the country's promise of freedom.

But, of course, war fever prevailed. The Senate cheered when Wilson called for war, a response that saddened Bob. Belle was in the gallery audience the next day when Bob shared the results of a referendum held in Monroe, Wisconsin, in which 954 had voted for peace and only 95 for war. He continued: "The sovereign power of the people never dies. It may be suppressed for a time, it may be misled, be fooled, silenced. . . . [But the people] will have their day and they will be heard. It will be as certain and as inevitable as the return of the tides, and as resistless, too." That night an effigy of Bob was burned in Texas. Later, when a newspaper reporter misquoted Bob as saying "we had no grievance with Germany" [he had said the opposite], the hatred spread to Wisconsin. More effigies of Bob were burnt. The school superintendents of Wisconsin petitioned the Senate to expel him promptly to "give the people of Wisconsin the right to hold up their heads without shame." Others also called for his ouster.

Belle found herself in the role of nursemaid, not only to her wounded warrior, but also to her son Robert Jr., who was severely ill with a strep infection. At the same time, the mortgage on the farm was in arrears and her son Phil was in financial trouble. Despite her family problems, she maintained her focus on the needless waste of life in Europe. The only bright spot on the horizon was the expectation that women's suffrage was inevitable; Belle had been active in the national suffrage campaign. In 1913, when the nineteenth amendment had been introduced, she had spoken before the relevant Senate committee. Later that year she and Elizabeth Evans promoted suffrage on the Chautauqua lecture circuit, a nationwide summer program of continuing education which traveled from city to city.

The holiday season of 1919 was sweet. The family reunited in Washington and invited friends in for an "old-fashioned party" with dancing and a sleepover. Peace had come in Europe—albeit under conditions both Belle and Bob abhorred—and women had the vote. Belle's anti-war efforts had not ended, however. She was elected president of a new anti-war organization, the Women's Committee for World Disarmament. Next year's Christmas found Belle in Washington again, this time speaking at a "Peace on Earth" march that she had helped to organize. In the freezing rain she declared to the crowd:

> We women have the power to compel disarmament. We need not plead or beg. We have the ballot. We propose to be practical. We propose to watch Congress. We vow to use our voices to defeat those who stand for militarism and war and to elect those who stand for peace and disarmament.

It was the *Voter's Hand-Book* strategy again. Belle continued to use her column to call for an international conference for disarmament. In 1922 her efforts, along with others', led to the first such conference in history, although the American delegation did not include a woman, as Belle had fiercely advocated.

In 1923 Bob and Belle toured post-war Europe. Their strongest impressions were of Germany. Belle wrote: "What was once a comfortable income now has the purchasing power of a few cents. These people must work long hours, or beg, or starve. They are actually disappearing. The increase in suicide is appalling." When he returned to the Senate, Bob proposed $10 million in hunger relief to Germany; his proposal was defeated.

The next year Belle stumped for Bob in his bid for the presidency on the Progressive ticket. She was the first woman to do this for a husband, and it brought her to a new level of recognition among the American public. She discussed politics as well as their relationship: "In all these years his opponents have tried to frighten the people with the bugaboo that he was too radical. . . . But the people kept right on electing him." And then, "I have been fortunate, marvelously lucky in having all these years a companion. True companionship is the greatest thing in the world."

In the end, the renegade reformer "Fighting Bob" La Follette received 17 percent of the popular vote, remarkable for a third-party candidate. But the campaign took its toll on his health. Over the course of a month, he suffered a series of heart attacks, for which there was no cure but "rest." He died at home in June 1925, surrounded by the family. In his final hours, Belle held his hand and spoke in an unending stream of her love for him and her vision of what his life's work had meant.

After the funeral Belle chose not to run for Bob's vacant Senate seat. She had never wanted to live in the public eye; besides, there was a better candidate: her son, Robert Jr., who had served as Bob's aide in recent years and who indeed won the seat. One also senses that Belle needed more time to grieve for her "true companion." She spent the last years of her life promoting Bob's legacy; writing a detailed, politically astute biography of him; and raising money to continue publishing *La Follette's Magazine*, now as the monthly, *The Progressive*. In 1931 Belle was halfway done writing the biography when she—who had never been seriously ill—suddenly died after her colon was punctured during a routine hospital exam. She was seventy-two.

In the November 1931 memorial edition of *The Progressive* magazine, Lincoln Steffens, a journalist and long-time friend of the family, wrote: "A great woman, this Belle La Follette, great as great men are great. She, too, was a statesman, politician, she could act, but she was content to beget action and actors." In her complex commitment to home, society, and government, he saw "tragedy," as many of Belle's biographers do. Belle probably wouldn't like that sentimental reading. Her being was fulfilled through action, through love and struggle. She buried none of her talents. As another friend of the family, Supreme Court Justice Louis Brandeis, once said, "The most important political office is that of the private citizen." Belle held that office, and much more.

HARRIET BELL MERRILL
1863–1915

Rolling to Rio

*H*arriet's brothers declared that what she proposed was "irresponsible."

"Irresponsible to whom?" Hattie replied.

"It is entirely out of the question for a petite little woman to hazard such a rigorous venture virtually on her own," said one.

The other asked her to wait a year, so that he could join her. "At the very least, I could carry the gun," he said.

Her brothers were not the only ones who questioned her plan to visit South America "solo." A well-meaning housemate brought up the issue of Mary Kingsley, the famous British explorer to Africa who had died from a tropical illness two years earlier. "The jungles are not a place for women in their forties," the housemate had informed Harriet, then thirty-nine.

One of her assistants in the University of Wisconsin labs had informed her that the climate was "fatal" to white people, adding, "and Wisconsin folks are the whitest I've ever seen."

Even her best friend and cousin Nora, who urged her to follow her dreams, had her doubts: "What is the concept in South

Harriet Bell Merrill

America regarding inoculating the populace and how in Sam Hill will you be protected against the bubonic plague, cholera or yellow fever?"

In contrast, Harriet's mentor and colleague at the University of Wisconsin, the zoologist Dr. Edward Asahel Birge, had promised her a supply of his finest silk nets, designed by him for catching microscopic crustaceans.

Indeed, collecting *Cladocera* ("water flea") specimens was the primary item on Harriet's agenda. She had been "fishing for Birge" ever since he began directing her master's degree work in 1891. The lure of these tiny creatures was associated with the birth of freshwater ecology, or "limnology," using the term coined in 1892. Their diversity in a given body of water was a sign of its aquatic health.

So, despite the many voices telling Harriet that she was too small, too weak, too white, too old, and definitely too female to travel to South America alone, she was determined to go. "I am intent in going solo on this journey as I have on all others, *but I will come home*, one way or another," she wrote to Nora in February of 1902.

In early July of that year, she was finally outbound on the SS *Byron*, a ship inhabited by large specimens from the order *Blattodea*—in other words, giant cockroaches. The ship was turned away at its first attempt to dock in Brazil because of bubonic plague quarantines. Regardless of such discomforts and dangers, Hattie wrote that the experience of "leaving the middle western university scene and sailing for South America was a release as liberating as loosing my corset stays and changing to a shift." Harriet's trip lasted over one year, and she returned to South America a second time, staying from 1907 to 1909. It is probable that her early death at age fifty-two was a consequence of tropical illnesses she contracted on her trips.

Harriet B. Merrill was born in Stevens Point, Wisconsin, in 1863—the same year that the University of Wisconsin admitted women to its student body. Her father, Samuel, belonged to a long-standing logging family from Brunswick, Maine. In 1858 Samuel followed the western logging boom to Portage County, Wisconsin, where the forest meets the prairie's eastern edge. There he met Anna Comstock Emmons, a "schoolmarm" from New York whose library was so extensive that he claimed he had to build extra rooms onto their Victorian house to contain all her books. These rooms, however, were soon filled with children, as Anna gave birth to two sons, Nathaniel and Roger, as well as daughter Harriet.

The wooded Wisconsin River was a favorite haunt of Harriet and her brothers. Of the siblings, it was she who was most drawn to nature. Harriet collected insects, rocks, and plants to examine at home with her microscope, while Nate played with his toy soldiers and Roger played music on his instruments. Harriet's self-taught scientific pursuits led her to wide-ranging observations of nature and helped to form her worldview. In the context of a discussion of Darwinism, she once wrote to her brother:

> When I focus on the most minute microorganism through a 1/250 power microscope and then view galaxies of "celestial cells" through a telescope, I feel that all material in the universe originated from the same basic cellular synthesis [and that] all of us is part of the Almighty. . . . I have maintained this thesis since our "tadpole days."

An excellent student, Harriet enrolled in the University of Wisconsin and graduated summa cum laude with a bachelor of science degree in 1890. In the decade that followed, she pursued her research zealously. She enrolled in Wisconsin's master of science program in the fall of 1890 and received her degree in 1893.

Research and temporary lectureships at Cornell and Chicago University led to an appointment in 1897 as the head of the science department of the new Milwaukee-Downer College, a women's college that had recently been formed from the merger of two long-established Wisconsin women's "seminaries," or colleges. Throughout the nineties she also served as the director of the physiology and biology departments at Milwaukee's East and South high schools.

It was in 1891, at the beginning of her work toward a master's degree in science, that Harriet received the inspiration that would determine her life's course. Dr. Edward A. Birge was a dynamic zoology professor at the university, with a reputation for almost ruthlessly high standards. In 1891 he had just become dean of the College of Letters and Sciences. He had done his graduate work in Massachusetts on the *Cladocera* order, and one day, according to Harriet, "he suggested that it would advance his work if I were to pick up where he left off 13 years ago." That is exactly what she did. In fact, it may have been her discovery of a rare specimen that enabled Birge to describe and name the *Bunops* genus in 1893.

Ten years later, Dean Birge became the acting president of the university and invited Harriet to return as an assistant professor to continue her—or their—studies. This invitation must have seemed to Harriet a vindication of her dedication as a scientist. Dean Birge had once told her that "advanced studies for women [are] wasted," as young women generally "look upon teaching as an occupation to fill the time between graduation and marriage." The thirty-eight-year-old Harriet could still boast of unmarried status. Furthermore, she had received professional honors beyond the Wisconsin master's degree, having received an honorary fellowship at Chicago University (1894–1897), and had enjoyed the opportunity to study at Woods Hole Institute in Massachusetts, at that time a rare privilege for a woman.

Harriet's first year as an assistant professor was incredibly taxing. What daytime hours were not dedicated to lecturing, she
spent, in her words, "fishing for Birge" on Wisconsin's lakes. She
occupied her evenings in the laboratory counting and cataloging
the microscopic specimens she had collected during the day. She
cheered herself with thoughts of the species' ecological importance: "I've never spent so much time on lakes, and when I try to
fathom why I pursue these 'water fleas,' I justify that they are essen-
tial to the food chain of the world's water supply—therefore—
LIFE!" Her cousin Nora, to whom she wrote this, was
unconvinced: "Forgive me for scolding, but I think too much is
expected of you. Can you never say NO!"

Of course, Harriet could not. Her situation as a woman scientist at the turn of the century required that she work more dili-
gently than her male colleagues to prove her worth. And even these
efforts could be misread by sexist assumptions. Some male scholars who were shown the credentials of "H. B. Merrill" were
impressed, until they were told "H. B." was a woman; they then
interpreted her dedication as "blind devotion" to Birge. Harriet
certainly admired and respected Birge and owed her position at
Wisconsin to him, but her letters show no sign of her depending
on him for her sense of self or purpose. Indeed, her later missives
to him demonstrated an egalitarian, collegial friendship, in which
she felt free to advise him about university politics, to which she
was, by necessity perhaps, keenly attuned.

Imagine, then, leaving this artificial "hothouse" atmosphere
for a one-year tour of a foreign continent with real rain forests!
Harriet had always dreamed of going to South America. Then, in
1901, her brother Roger sent her a copy of Rudyard Kipling's
story "The Beginning of the Armadillos," which ended with a
poem. The refrain captured Harriet's imagination: "Oh, I'd love to
roll to Rio / Someday before I'm old." The phrase "roll to Rio"

began appearing in her letters to friends and family throughout 1901. Harriet clearly saw how her headlong pursuit of the microscopic *Cladocera* could now justify a year's sojourn abroad.

Specimens were not all she pursued, however. Harriet was keen on recording the cultural, political, economic, and historical features of the lands to which she traveled. Assuming the role of the plucky female correspondent, held previously by women such as Nellie Bly, she reported back regularly to the *Milwaukee Sentinel*, which published more than thirty separate articles sent by her, along with photographs. She also sent letters containing information of interest to the Milwaukee Public Museum and to history departments at universities with which she had been associated, and collected objects ranging from water fleas to giant insects and native lacework for the museum. All this, as well as leaning over the edges of boats collecting water flea samples, and hustling them back to the lab for cataloging!

Harriet's writing style in the *Sentinel* articles reveals a lively mind with a wide range of interests. The articles range widely in topic—from business opportunities for Wisconsinites to styles in clothing. "H. B.," as she signed her stories, emerges as a woman who sees herself with a good deal of humor, despite her quite serious pursuit of science. Here is one example of the stories told in this vein:

> On the riverboat, I was followed about by a cheerful Guarani [native Indian] boy. He was fascinated with my note-taking but absolutely puzzled by my "fishing nets." For that matter, so were the passengers. . . . One morning when I left the boat to go to Lake San Bernadino, the Indian boy came to help me carry the equipment needed to catch the 1.1 millimeter elusive Bunops "animal." As I walked down the gangway,

holding aloft Dr. Birge's fine silk nets like banners, and the Guarani boy tagging behind with a box of little bottles, I think the boat might have keeled over from the weight of every man on board leaning over the starboard side—gawking with curiosity over what could possibly be my catch of the day!

Harriet's writings also played upon cultural differences between the United States and Latin America. She was particularly attentive to differences in the roles and proper costume of women:

Since I was the guest of honor [at a provincial governor's mansion in Argentina], I arrived early in what I considered my best traveling ensemble (boots and all). Typical of the elegant wealthy South American women, the Governor's wife and daughters were attired in silks, satins and opulent jewelry—some with stones as large as those seen in museums. Then, before the other guests gathered, the family quickly changed into their plainest cotton street clothes, tactfully making me seem less understated in costume!

In her letters to Nora, Harriet more bluntly noted that it appeared the custom of Latin men "to dominate their womenfolk completely," and reported having to fend off a few clumsy passes made at her. A more amusing note to her brother concerned an army barracks she had to pass on the way from the laboratory at the University of Brazil to the room where she was staying. Once, as she passed, the men who were drilling saluted her, crying in unison, "La chiquita Enriqueta!" She had become a local sensation.

Five-foot Harriet walked everywhere in her practical, masculine boots with low heels and broad soles. On her collecting treks into the interior, she carried a heavy camera, "fishing" nets and bottles for specimens, and sometimes even a gun. Then she dipped her nets into the water and collected invisible animals in jars! That she became a sensation was inevitable.

Arguably her most interesting letter was one written to Nora about the Brazilian bacteriologist Oswaldo Cruz. Harriet never married and—by all accounts—didn't want to. Nonetheless, forty-year-old Harriet was not immune to sexual feelings. She begins the letter, "At last I have met someone who epitomizes all that I find intellectually stimulating as well as physically attractive in a man." By her description, Cruz was tall and slender and moved with physical grace; Hattie could barely stand the intensity of eye contact with him. Cruz's mission was to eradicate yellow fever in Brazil, and he had made significant progress by inspiring medical students to gain experience in the field by producing serum and inoculating villagers in disease-ridden parts of the country. Best of all, Cruz listened with great interest to Harriet's description of her work. As she wrote, almost luridly, "I felt it a pity that he is married. It is no surprise that he has six children." By the close of the letter, she forced herself "back to earth" and to proper feminist priorities: "I understand I am to meet some outstanding women doctors and will write about it for the *Milwaukee Sentinel*."

Harriet loved the tropical rain forest but always took care to note that nothing in the tropics could compare to the beauty of North American forests. She noted with interest the extravagant wealth of her hosts but also pointed out the unjust class disparity upon which it was based. Possibly her most memorable experience in South America was her visit to the Rio de Janeiro Botanical Gardens, where exotic birds and giant butterflies flew unfettered by cages. She had never imagined such a gorgeous scene existed, and it impressed itself permanently on her mind.

Harriet returned to South America in 1907 and remained there until 1909, re-establishing her contacts and focusing more intensely on building the South American specimen collection. While her 1902–1903 efforts had yielded 71 samples, her 1907–1909 expedition yielded over 600 samples, each with dozens of different species to sort, count, and catalog.

Did Harriet contract a tropical disease on her second trip to South America? It is certain that during this more extended stay she came into contact with more bodies of standing water, in more out-of-the-way locales. She was not diagnosed with any disease except "heart trouble," but her symptoms sound like Chagas' disease, discovered in Brazil in 1909 and still the leading cause of heart failure in the world. The disease is caused by a protozoan parasite transmitted by insect bites, and can take years to manifest itself in its victims. In 1914 Harriet was seriously weakened by "heart troubles." Nevertheless, in spite of her illness, or perhaps because of it, she decided to pursue her lifelong dream of earning a doctorate at the University of Illinois at Urbana-Champaign. (Wisconsin's zoology department did not offer such a degree.) Here, her life returned into focus, as she recorded her doings and observations in twice-weekly letters to Dr. Birge; her letters also included a good measure of gossip concerning public figures at midwestern universities.

As usual, her schedule was loaded up with sections to teach and labs to run, along with classes about subjects that, given her lifelong focus on aquatic species and ecosystems, struck her as useless. Ironically, the one she complained most about was a course on parasites ("I shall die of parasitology"). She also quipped about what she felt was the excessively religious culture of the community and college, which denied all access to laboratories on Sundays except to "feed animals," a loophole Harriet took full advantage of.

Even in September, Harriet's health was tentative, and those who cared for her knew it, despite her best efforts to make light of the situation. One letter finds her apologizing to Birge, who had evidently complained about her insouciant attitude, then adding, "but I was so decidedly lame, halt, and blind that [my condition did seem] a little funny." When winter came, Harriet's health and spirits plummeted along with the temperature, and she remained bed-ridden for weeks. The rooming house where she stayed was seedy, serving food that was "dirty and spoiled" and depriving its residents of heat. In December alone, the pipes burst three times.

In January she was admitted to the hospital, where the medicine administered to her caused vivid dreams. Most of Harriet's dreams were of South America. Here is one she recorded in a letter to her niece, Marie:

> The other night I was in a consulate dining room. A housemaid was wrapping the best silver in cloths with camphor to prevent the extreme tropical humidity from tarnishing the pieces between their usage. I happened to see my reflection in an ornate mirror above a console. It was eerie. The silver backed mirror, cloudy with tarnishing showed a tattered image, while elegant young women in their high-heeled slippers clicked past me on the marble floor in the foyer. I was awakened by a nurse who had placed a poultice, heavy with the scent of eucalyptus, on my chest.

Perhaps in the back of Harriet's mind was the thought of who she might have been—a beautiful woman who seeks and attracts men. Now in her fifties, she wrote, "I am hoping that one evening I might be back in the ballroom of a governor's mansion, attired in such a way that I might be asked to dance." Though she had never before had "the desire to glide across a floor," she allowed herself the fantasy of dancing with Dr. Cruz, or Señor Lopez, the handsome son of a general who guided her around Paraguay and intrigued her with his progressive ideas. This "alternative Harriet" would perhaps have been one who was, like the "best silver" in the dream, carefully protected from the moist air and the diseases that it fostered.

But the real Harriet, in the end, had no regrets. In February she was brought back to Milwaukee, where she was in and out of hospital care for two months. On April 3 she wrote to her cousin Nora, thanking her for visiting, and the flowers she brought.

> I look at the flowers and remember the gardens in Rio. The Avenue of Royal Palms, the giant ferns, the tropical butterflies, like masses of fluttering blossoms. All of the species seemed so very free in that symbiotic paradise. There were no wire boundaries in the garden conservatory. My hope is that the magnificent specimens can continue their escape—from being captured and put in cases in the museums. I keep trying to escape. I will fly with my boots on!

One week later, she had flown. The year was 1915.

For decades Harriet's achievements were largely forgotten, until the granddaughter of her brother inherited a box of her personal papers and photographs as part of her grandmother's estate. This fortuitous inheritance gave Harriet back to the world. In 1990 a building at the University of Wisconsin's Trout Lake Research Station was named after "H. B." Merrill.

LILLIE ROSA MINOKA-HILL
1876–1952

"She Who Carries Aid"

*W*hen Lillie Rosa Minoka-Hill arrived at the Episcopal Church at Oneida that Thanksgiving Day in 1949, she was not entirely certain what was to take place. She had worn her best dress, as she had been told she was to receive an honor of some kind. She wondered if it would be like the prize she had received just a couple months before. In September she had taken the train all the way to Chicago, where she was named "Indian of the Year." Rosa smiled at the memory. It was good to be recognized for her work. It was even better to be recognized as an Indian, even though she had never lived among her own people, the Mohawks.

The Oneida tribal leaders ushered her into the parish hall. This was different from the Chicago ceremony; the crowd of 150 that greeted her was made up of her patients! As she passed through their midst on the way up to the rostrum, she sensed rather than saw who they were, her failing eyesight blending their faces with those of their relations—the children she had delivered and the grandparents laid to rest.

The tribal leaders fastened a band of wampum around her

Lillie Rosa Minoka-Hill

white-haired head. Wampum, she reflected, was the symbol of honor shared by the People of the Longhouse, the Haudenosaunee or Iroquois, including the Mohawk and Oneida alike. As she heard the words being spoken about her, a flood of memories passed through her mind: the long, grueling childbirths she had assisted, the wounds she had bound, the desperate journeys she had taken through snow and mud. And yes, the deaths she had witnessed, from diphtheria, typhoid, influenza, and tuberculosis.

It had become silent in the church. A pipe was lit and made its way down the line to her. Her hands trembled as she took it. Her old thoughts returned—the ones that had plagued her throughout her life: Am I worthy? Do I belong? As she held the ceremonial pipe to her lips, the questions seemed to lose their power.

The pipe was passed back to the speaker. He held it up as he spoke. "With this pipe and the sacred willow plant you have made smoke. And this smoke will waft upward to the dwelling of the Great God. And the Great God will be pleased and say, 'Welcome, my child.'"

As he continued, she began to understand. They were adopting her into the tribe. Her new name was *Youdagent*, "She Who Carries Aid." Forty years passed in a heartbeat, and she was a bride again, coming to the Oneida reservation with Charles. Another thirty years fell away, and she was a child, coming home to a family she had never met.

Seventy-one-year-old Rosa responded with great pain. "I feel very humble at this great honor. I am happy that I now can call you my brothers, sisters, nieces and nephews."

The hush that had held the room broke, and Rosa felt her burden rise, with the willow smoke, to the heavens.

* * *

Lillie Minnetoga's mother was a Mohawk from St. Regis, in the northeastern part of New York along the Saint Lawrence River. A remnant of the Mohawk nation still lives there, on either side of the Quebec border. It is not known how her mother met Dr. Joshua Gibbons Allen, a bachelor from Philadelphia. In the 1870s, when Lillie was born, some Eastern Woodland Indians were making a living selling traditional Indian craftwork, such as basketry, in the large eastern cities. It may be that Lillie's grandmother was engaged in such work. When Lillie's mother reached the age of fourteen, she may have become a domestic servant, as Native American girls with no other means of support often did. This is the most likely circumstance for the intimate meeting that led to her pregnancy.

Dr. Allen was an obstetrician who served part-time at the "lying-in" charity hospital in Philadelphia, a place where unmarried women went to "hide their shame." In the Victorian society of the 1800s, most babies born in such hospitals were abandoned to orphanages while their mothers became wet nurses for wealthy women. Dr. Allen may have brought Lillie's mother there for prenatal care or for delivery, or both. He wanted to do his duty by God, but he by no means wished to relinquish his standing in the community.

The death of Lillie's mother in childbirth left her identity—and the exact nature of her relationship to Dr. Allen—a mystery to all but the doctor. Until she was five Lillie lived with her Mohawk grandmother in a tent or cottage in Atlantic City, a growing resort town. In adulthood she remembered her grandmother as being a loving person, almost spoiling her. Every so often the portly, white Quaker man from Philadelphia would visit. One day he told Lillie to say goodbye to her grandmother, then took her by the hand and led her away from the tent. They took the train to

Philadelphia, with Lillie playing the little "wooden Indian," facing straight ahead to avoid the stares of strangers.

The final destination for "Rosa"—as she was renamed—was the four-story brick house of Jane and Israel Grahame, a Quaker couple who ran a small school and housed a few boarders such as Rosa. They were gentle, loving people with whom Rosa corresponded long after she left their institute. Rosa's fate was far different from that of Native American children removed from reservations to attend military-style boarding schools, where they were forcefully stripped of their identity, physically abused, and informed of their "racial inferiority."

Notwithstanding her relative good fortune, Rosa's confusion about her identity caused her heartache. Jane Grahame called her "my Little Gypsy" or "my Little Mohawk daughter." Rosa read stories about Indians from books that Dr. Allen brought her, and at one point she memorized and recited the entire text of Longfellow's epic poem "Hiawatha," which romanticizes the inevitable disappearance of the Indians of the northeast. As she grew older, she changed her surname from "Minnetoga" to "Minneoka," and later to "Minoka": The significance of these changes remains obscure. She also began using the initial "L." before her name. At age thirteen she was placed at a guardian's house in Quebec to study French. Upon her return she announced her conversion to Catholicism, the adopted religion of most Mohawks at that time.

With this upstream journey of cultural self-discovery came a realization of her individual talents. She had performed well in the rigorous academic environment of the Grahame school. She also discovered a "natural bent" for taking care of people and began to imagine a future for herself as a nurse. However, her benefactor, the mysterious Dr. Allen—the man who had known her mother, yet refused to talk about her—encouraged her to become a doctor instead. Nursing, he thought, would be too taxing physically for her, and she could handle the intellectual challenge of medical school. Whether to satisfy his or her own desires, she enrolled in the Women's Medical College of Philadelphia in 1895, at the age of eighteen. There, just before her classes began, Dr. Allen revealed his identity to her. He was not merely her benefactor, as the public believed; he was her father. Also, perhaps to ease her mind, he assured her that she was not illegitimate.

"L. Rosa Minoka" formed close friendships with fellow students at the Women's Medical College, some of which lasted a lifetime. The school attracted women with strong spirits, diverse backgrounds, and commitment to service. Many of its graduates became missionaries, the one medical career women were then encouraged to pursue. Some of the students had their origins in disadvantaged communities and planned to return—be it to China, Syria, or the African-American ghetto—to provide service to those who otherwise would receive none. In this atmosphere Rosa began to imagine her future of service to native populations in Puerto Rico or Mexico or the American Southwest. She did not think of St. Regis or other Mohawk settlements. By this time in her life, she may have felt more comfortable in the role of outsider.

At the same time, she sought out friendships with other American Indians. In college she socialized with students from two Indian boarding schools, Carlisle Institute and the Lincoln Institute. Their stories probably served to illuminate her own. These friendships continued after she graduated from medical college in 1899. She and her best friend, Frances Bartlett, set up offices side-by-side in downtown Philadelphia for walk-in clients, while they searched for hard-to-find internships. In 1902 Rosa won an internship at the Women's Hospital in Philadelphia. That same year she met nineteen-year-old Anna Hill, an Oneida student at the Lincoln Institute, and through Anna, her future husband.

Anna's brother, Charles Abram Hill, was a few years older than Rosa. He was a handsome, charismatic man who played baseball and the cornet, but he was painfully conscious of racism and frustrated by his treatment as an "Injun." At Carlisle, the director's motto had been "Kill the Indian and save the man." The studies there prepared him only for industrial or agricultural jobs, where he inevitably was paid less than the other workers. He dreamed of going home to his family's land allotment on the Oneida reservation. Rosa was immediately attracted to him. She wrote him requesting another meeting, with or without his sister, then confessed over the phone that there were things "she couldn't say to him" in Anna's company. Rosa stood out from his many other girlfriends, perhaps because of the challenge posed by her cultivated mind and complex personality.

Charles awakened a love in Rosa that was so intense that it threw her whole self into doubt once more. In the letters written during their courtship, she persistently questioned whether she was worthy of his love. She felt that because she had been "rescued," she did not deserve personal happiness but should do her part to serve instead. She feared that Charles would reject her once he knew her "secret." Tunnel-minded by habit, Rosa often failed to understand the playful hints that Charles used to ask for affection—or corrected him when he misspoke, then castigated herself later when she realized how insensitive she'd been. On the other hand she must have sensed that this rational persona of hers had helped her and would help her survive. Her intellectual training was the part of herself she owed to Dr. Allen.

Then, in September 1903, Dr. Allen died. Just prior to his death a small notice in the newspaper made public his paternity of Rosa. His will also acknowledged her as his daughter. One crucial fact was left untold, however: the identity of Rosa's mother. Rosa waited as his estate was sorted out, anxious for the discovery of a letter directed to her, which he had promised would be among his papers. No such letter was ever found. Several weeks later, she wrote to Charles, finally revealing what she knew about her birth. More intimately, she explained how she always felt she had two identities, the one cheerful and dutiful and eager to please, and the other, less pliant—even harsh in nature. She felt that she had been "deceiving" him all along.

This personal "confession" gave Rosa new freedom to love Charles. They began talking of marriage in earnest, although Charles had very little money. The settling of Dr. Allen's estate solved that problem; he left the majority of his modest wealth to Rosa, in a trust fund. Religion proved one more hurdle: Rosa requested that Charles, who was raised in the Episcopal Church, convert to Catholicism (he did not) and demanded that their children be raised Catholic (they were). Charles returned home to Wisconsin and began building a two-story house, catching up on reservation politics, and starting a farming operation on the family allotment. In June 1905, Rosa and Charles were married in Philadelphia, and in October, they arrived by train at the Oneida station as an Oneida band played for them. Rosa had never been out of the city; she had never seen such beautiful country as that of northern Wisconsin. Charles's grandmother showed her the native plants, roots, and wildflowers used as remedies by the Oneida. Rosa would have known some of the names, such as digitalis (foxglove), from her scientific medical training. Other herbal remedies she would adopt as they proved effective. At first, she treated only members of Charles's extended family: A person would come to her kitchen or front steps and sit awhile chatting. Then he or she would announce, "I'm your relation," and Rosa would understand that the person sought medical advice.

Rosa welcomed these visits. It had remained cloudy in her discussions with Charles whether or not she would continue to practice medicine. The farm required a great deal of work, and Charles wanted to start a family. There was a young Oneida doctor on the reservation, recently trained at Marquette Medical School; she did not want to cause trouble with him. Furthermore, it would be illegal for her to practice without obtaining a license in Wisconsin, a procedure she wished to avoid. But Charles could hardly expect her to refuse service to his relatives or friends; and if she did not charge money for services, the law would take no interest in her.

Rosa was a champion of preventative medicine: a balanced diet, exercise, and eschewal of alcohol. When a person was sick, however, she preferred to prescribe pharmaceutical drugs, which she received through the mail from her female doctor friends in Philadelphia, simply because the quantities of substances were better controlled. She never discouraged a patient from using a traditional remedy; she simply suggested they try her medicine in addition to theirs. These strategies for accomplishing cures without roiling the tribal waters were all part of what she later called her "inconspicuous way."

Rosa traveled to Philadelphia for the birth of her first child. There was good reason to be leery of the reservation hospital, which lacked an operating room, a laboratory, and even a laundry. As a physician and as one whose own mother died in childbirth, she was aware of all the things that could go wrong. Rosa named her daughter "Rosa Melissa." For her subsequent deliveries, Rosa was less cautious. Over the next few years, she gave birth to three sons, Charles Allen, Norbert, and Alfred Grahame, then, at the age of thirty-nine, to twin daughters, Josephine and Jane Frances. All were healthy and all were baptized in the Catholic Church. Despite the distractions of a house full of babies, Rosa continued to subscribe to medical journals and treat the relatives who presented their cases in her kitchen.

Charles worked hard on the farm and played cornet in the Episcopal Church band on Sundays. In 1916 he began to notice a "stitch" in his side. One spring morning while fishing Duck Creek with his son, the pain grew so intense he had to lie down and curl up. It began to snow. The boy dashed home to Rosa, who hitched up the horses to take her husband where he needed to go. As she reached the scene and spoke with him, she knew he had appendicitis. If only he had told her of his pain, if only she hadn't been too preoccupied; if only she had been trained in surgery! They set out for the Catholic hospital at Green Bay, stopping for the night at a patient's house. The operation the following day could not save him. He died on Easter Sunday, and Rosa's heart broke.

What followed was "as tough a time as she ever had." Rosa had six children to raise, all but one under the age of six; animals to feed; crops to plant, harvest, and "put up"; and last but not least, patients to tend. America's entry into World War I took the Oneida doctor away and brought his patients to her. Influenza ravaged the home front. All of Rosa's children were sick, as was she. (Several years later, her eldest daughter would die of the illness while at a boarding school in Fond du Lac.) Throughout the winter of 1917–1918, all Rosa could do was keep the pot-bellied stove burning day and night, and pray that the "gifts" people brought in exchange for treatment would keep her children fed. Her trust fund paid for the medicines she bought for patients at the pharmacy in Green Bay. As the children grew older, they contributed to the running of the household by hunting for squirrels and birds on their way home from the Catholic grade school they attended.

After the war Dr. Frances Bartlett, then married, visited Rosa at Oneida and encouraged her friend to return east to practice medicine there. Given the comforts of city living, it must have been a suggestion Rosa took seriously, but she was needed exactly where she was. The Oneida doctor had been killed in the war, and she had been serving an ever-widening circle of clients. The community continued to battle influenza. Denied access to hospitals and proper health education, American Indians during that period had a child mortality rate three times that of the national population. Furthermore, if Rosa abandoned the Hills' "allotment" of land, it would likely cede to white ownership. Not only would her children lose their inheritance by moving to the city, they would lose their culture, as she had. Rosa decided to stay in Oneida

It was not easy to balance the demands of her patients and her children. In many cases she had to put her profession first, abandoning her children at all hours to attend to emergencies, sometimes staying whole days away from home. On the one hand her circumstances necessitated this choice; without a man farming full-time, both she and the children depended upon her patients to remember their needs at slaughter- or harvest-time. On the other hand the choice was probably unconscious. Growing up without a family's love, in Quaker schools that emphasized "doing good," Rosa followed the path she knew best. Her "inconspicuous way" of giving to others without demanding immediate payment was fundamentally an Indian way, a fact that must have deepened her satisfaction in her work.

Finally, during the Depression, Rosa obtained a license from the state medical examining board, legally enabling her to charge patients. The stock market crash had dried up her trust fund, making it impossible for her to stock medicine, and one of the twins needed tuition for nursing school. It cost her one hundred dollars and a flurry of paperwork between various points in Pennsylvania and Wisconsin to become licensed. The license expanded her authority to refer patients and prescribe medicines, and it got her a job as a local health officer, with an office in town, separate from her home. She used a sliding scale for fees, still accepting goods for payment when someone lacked money. She served white patients as well as Native Americans. A patient described her bedside manner from that period:

> She just knows you. She probably did know us ever since we were born, and she . . . called everybody by their name. She had a smooth [*sic*] and kindness in her speech, to the point, and in that mixture there, you sensed that authority that you had to respect, that authority that was there. . . . It took a few minutes and you got the feeling that she had known you forever.

In 1946 Rosa experienced a heart attack that left her blind in one eye. She continued practicing—from her home now—in order to pay for food and other necessities. She received press coverage in many of the state newspapers in the summer of 1949 when she traveled to Atlantic City to receive the "Doctor of the Year" award at the American Medical Association convention. In her speech she laid forth the facts about the inadequacy of health services provided to Native Americans. During the same trip she attended the fifty-year reunion of her class at the Women's Medical College and saw her friends for one last time.

Rosa died in 1952, after saying good-bye to all but one of her children. Two years later, the church community erected a granite monument in the center of Oneida in memory of Rosa. On that day, a crowd of 1,500 gathered to remember the doctor who "carried aid" to the reservation.

ELSA ULBRICHT
1885–1980

Artist with a Cause

*N*ovember 6, 1935, had arrived. Approximately 250 formerly unemployed women arrived at the westside Veterans Administration office, where the Milwaukee Handicrafts Project had rented two rooms. Elsa Ulbricht knew of these women as names on a list—more specifically, names at the bottom of the list of eligible participants for Works Progress Administration employment. Anyone with skills of any kind had already been selected by other local WPA projects, such as those in construction and the arts. Those who remained were not just unemployed; they were virtually unemployable—destitute women, ranging in age from twenty to seventy, who had never held at a job in their lives. They showed up at the VA wearing tattered clothes and downcast expressions, learned from standing in long relief lines. Many seemed weak from malnourishment.

Elsa feared for the success of her project, but she immediately sensed that these women's fears were greater. They had more at stake. If they could not perform the work adequately—or if this project failed, as some inevitably did—they would go back on the

Elsa Ulbricht with former Wisconsin governor Warren Knowles

dole, and their households would return to hunger, deprivation, and shame.

Elsa had taken on the project at the invitation of her friend Harriet Clinton, the district director of WPA projects. As a *Sentinel* reporter, Harriet had covered Elsa's forays into experimental drama, dance, and crafts education. Coincidentally, Elsa had been developing a similar idea to present to her friend. Together, they won the approval of the president of the Milwaukee State Teachers' College, where Elsa taught. Officials of Milwaukee County readily agreed to participate, as expanded employment in WPA programs meant fewer mouths for them to feed.

Elsa and Harriet did not always share the same vision for the project, however. Harriet imagined women being put to work cutting out pictures from leftover scraps of wallpaper, a notion Elsa rejected in no uncertain terms. If she were to direct such a program, the crafts that were manufactured must be useful and beautiful, not the products of federally-funded "busy-work." Trained artists should design products such as toys, books, or furniture needed by public institutions; the unskilled workers would then make these goods in quantity using simple production techniques. The federal government would pay salaries and wages. Expenditures for materials and rented space could be recouped in the sales of the high-quality items, priced "at cost." All would benefit in terms of jobs and experience, and the public taste would be elevated by exposure to quality design. Quality would be the key to the program's success.

On November 6, 1935, this vision seemed out of reach. When scissors were distributed to the women, it became obvious that some had never used them before. The only other supplies the project heads had managed to gather were a few stacks of magazines and paper and paste. Thus, the new employees of the Milwaukee Handicrafts Project were doing much of what Harriet had envisioned and Elsa abhorred: cutting pictures out of magazines to bind into books for public hospitals, kindergartens, and nursery schools. Elsa and her staff patiently circulated through the rooms, providing much-needed words of encouragement.

At the end of this first day, Harriet had one more question. Would Elsa be willing to take on blacks? Unemployed black women had been denied participation in many of the other WPA programs. Elsa's answer was an unequivocal "yes." Over the course of that week, participation in the Handicrafts Project swelled from 250 to 900, as black women signed up for the new work opportunity. Elsa and her helpers would have to hustle to find space, materials, and assignments for all of those who needed work in Depression-era Milwaukee. They couldn't—and they wouldn't!—cut and paste pictures forever!

Elsa Emile Ulbricht was 100 percent German-American. Both sets of grandparents were German immigrants, frontier settlers of Milwaukee. The relative of whom she spoke most often was her maternal grandfather, Henry Buestrin, who arrived in Milwaukee with his parents in 1841. Henry's approach to life was "experimental," one of Elsa's favorite words. As a contractor, he worked for the love of the work rather than for the money, opting for jobs that represented unique engineering challenges while charging his clients just enough to cover expenses. He was known for moving houses and performing other difficult and important jobs—such as repairing underwater cables—that no one else knew how to approach. According to Elsa, her mother, Augusta Buestrin, inherited his "good common sense." Augusta married Oswald Ulbricht, a lumber dealer, who built the family a handsome home on North 28th Street. Elsa lived there virtually her whole life, from the age of nine to ninety.

Elsa's artistic talent emerged early. One day in elementary school, she drew a daisy that was so beautiful that her teacher asked her to paint a border of such daisies around the perimeter of the room. Like a diminutive Michelangelo painting the Sistine Chapel ceiling, she complained of a stiff neck and cramped fingers, "but in the end I still loved daisies, as I do to this day," she said later, at age seventy.

After graduating from high school, Elsa entered the program for kindergarten education at the Milwaukee Normal School. She read much of Friedrich Froebel's work and sympathized wholly with his emphasis on play and the physical world, but not at all with the regimentation of his system. Elsa was keen on breaking rules during her college years, smoking cigarettes in public simply because women weren't supposed to do so, and dancing bare-legged in Milwaukee's Lake Park with a "Terpsichore" troupe that wore scandalously "diaphanous" gowns. She also bobbed her hair ten years before it became fashionable.

Clearly, Elsa was an unforgettable student. She had a knack for being asked to teach at schools she had once attended. In 1907 Elsa was hired at the same kindergarten that she had attended as a five-year-old. With the encouragement of one of her Normal School teachers, she began attending evening art courses at the Wisconsin School of Art, recently founded by Alexander Mueller. Five years later, two of which were spent studying art in New York, Elsa was offered a job at Mueller's renamed School of Applied and Fine Arts, which had recently formed a partnership with Elsa's other alma mater, the Milwaukee Normal School. The art school became part of the renamed Milwaukee State Teachers' College, which, a couple of mergers later, became the University of Wisconsin at Milwaukee.

From 1911 to 1956 Elsa taught art techniques to future schoolteachers. Before her hiring, there was no "normal" training in arts in Wisconsin—in other words, no teacher training in art. This gave Elsa the role she most relished: that of creative groundbreaker. She saw the "applied arts" or crafts as the natural direction for children's art education. Thus, she began with a course in weaving, the craft practiced by her mother, and followed it with a course in bookbinding, which she had recently learned at a seminar at the Hull House in Chicago. One after the next, she designed courses in puppetry, basketry, and screen-printing. In Elsa's words, the hiring of new teachers to take over her more established courses "was very much to my liking because then I could experiment on something else."

At the same time, Elsa was experimenting in the community, as an active member of Players Theater. Founded by Laura Sherry in 1909 to present intimate, noncommercial and experimental theater to Milwaukee's public, it was the first such "little theater" in the nation. Besides acting in productions, including at least one male role, Elsa dove into the technical aspects of stagecraft: set design, costuming, make-up, choreography, and direction. She subsequently worked many of these crafts into the Normal School arts curriculum.

The beginning of Elsa's art career coincided with the height of the Arts and Crafts movement, which had started in England in the 1870s, migrated to America in the 1890s, and found its greatest resonance in the Midwest in the decades that followed. Founded on the principle that beauty and usefulness could be combined, the movement was also strongly egalitarian. Gustav Stickley, an early Arts and Crafts proponent in America, championed "a form of industrial education which will develop self-reliance and initiative and foster creative ability, so that men and women alike will be able to earn their own living under any and all circumstances, and to do the best work that is in them." The year that Elsa began teaching crafts, 1911, Frank Lloyd Wright, that most famous exemplar of the movement, began his lifelong project of building a home, "Taliesin," in Spring Green, Wisconsin. As usual, Elsa was in step with the leaders in the arts. In 1916 she helped found the Wisconsin Society of Applied Arts, whose mission it was to promote the crafts, raise the standards of beauty for commonplace objects, and improve cooperation between designers and workers.

It was this ethic that Elsa brought to the Milwaukee Handicrafts Project. Without it, the project would never have attained the fame it did, nor would its products have had the same high-quality, stylized appeal. Many of the objects crafted by the project workshops now belong to museum collections, while others remained in use for decades by the institutions that originally purchased them. Still, despite Elsa's initial insistence on the quality of the products, it was the human dimension that emerged as the project's greatest triumph and her greatest joy.

During her supervision of the Handicrafts Project, Elsa never quit her job at the State Teachers' College. In fact, because of her college salary, she could direct the project on a purely volunteer basis, which she felt gave her the right to circumvent some of the more senseless federal regulations, such as the WPA's ban on visitors to work sites. On a typical day she would start her classes at the college, then tell her students, "Well, I'm going to have to go, you'll have to be on your own." In a characteristic quip, she later professed that the students learned more when she was not there, because "they were on their mettle, you see." Elsa had never believed in "prodding" students; it was up to each one to discover their personal connection to the work.

Moreover, Elsa was providing $75-a-month jobs for talented State College graduates who otherwise would have been unemployed in the Depression economy. The "foreman-assistants," as they were known, enjoyed the work immensely. Their jobs were challenging and deeply rewarding; there was "no clock watching," as one of them put it. In the grand spirit of experimentation that Elsa inspired, these young artists were constantly designing new products in new media and subjecting them to scrutiny. If the items did not pass muster, they were simply scrapped.

At the same time, the foreman-assistants worked with people who were discovering capabilities they had not known they possessed. Worker morale became the central tenet of Elsa's administration; if the project failed to produce happier, healthier human beings, it had failed. To empower the workers, she established an elected workers' council to help set policies, handle discipline, and organize social functions. After the first month's $50 paycheck, many of the workers went to hairdressers for permanent waves. Elsa rejoiced at this sign that the women's pride in themselves was beginning to awaken.

The types of work in the Handicrafts Project proliferated in creative abundance, as the project eventually expanded to occupy two floors of a vacated factory building, covering two entire blocks of downtown Milwaukee. After binding scrapbooks, the women began binding other papers, such as county records, into books. Eventually, they produced books in Braille for the Institution for the Blind in Janesville. They also produced boxed sets of instructions for bookbinding, so that schoolteachers could introduce the craft to their students. Simultaneously, they began block printing, first on paper to illustrate books, then on fabric. Eventually, boldly decorative curtains were made from the block prints. From scraps of fabric, the workers made patchwork quilts for nursery schools, and wall hangings. From old wool uniforms and blankets, they made hook rugs, a skill many of the women took up in their own homes. For each of these products, they had specific patterns to follow.

Then the doll unit began. The dolls were tremendously popular. After much experimentation to perfect the molded parts, production began. Quite spontaneously, black dolls appeared in production along with white dolls, and whenever a white doll was given to a school or hospital, a black one accompanied it. Some of the workers took home the patterns for doll clothing and adapted them to fit their own children. A line of "costume dolls" representing the traditional dress of different nationalities became popular; recent immigrants in the project provided the expertise. Eventually, these innovations led to the development of historically correct costumes for high school drama departments.

By the time the project was manufacturing toys, men had been invited to join, many of them carpenters out of work. Wooden toys such as puzzle boards, trains, and building blocks were designed "in an educational way," with sturdy moving parts and several coats of lead-free paint. Then the carpenters turned to creating mission-style furniture, upholstered with different block-printed fabrics from the project. Finally, the project took up weaving. For this, Elsa and two men collaborated in designing various-sized four-harness looms, which workers then produced. Birch-wood looms as well as woven goods were added to the extensive catalog of items from which institutions could order. Institutions could also custom-order articles they desired. Soon, the project was selling as many products to institutions outside Wisconsin as to those within the state.

Copycat projects appeared around the nation, and Elsa welcomed them with some amusement. Her philosophy was that "we can do more, we can do better." She realized early, however, that her facility and zest for "shifting gears" was not shared by all the workers. Many preferred to stick to a job once they'd learned it. This challenge was easily met by hiring new employees. Between 1935 and 1943, the project employed 5,000 Milwaukee residents. A few of them excelled at the work and were promoted to the design staff. Many of them moved on to employment in private industry, particularly in the growing defense industries.

Elsa received many letters from project "graduates," thanking her for the new life they had gained. One incident shows how a woman was empowered by association with the project to imagine a larger civic role for herself. A black woman named Hanie came to Elsa's home early one morning. The 1848 house Hanie was renting was scheduled for demolition; it seemed a shame to her that such a vintage structure should be destroyed. Elsa took the issue to Harriet Clinton, and with the help of the Historical Society, the house was moved to Esterbrook Park on the Upper Eastside. Then, the project replicated historic wallpaper and period furniture, and they turned the home into a museum that stayed functional for at least two decades. Elsa was particularly charmed by a red, plush photograph album featuring photographs of Hanie and herself in period clothing, as the fictional "family" of the house.

At one point, Eleanor Roosevelt visited the project, and was sufficiently impressed to feature it in one of her "My Day" columns. She also carried a set of Milwaukee dolls with her on her WPA speaking tours as examples of the program's success. In the early 1940s, when the project faced extinction due to growing defense budgets, it was to Mrs. Roosevelt that Elsa turned for help. In a letter, she appealed to an expanded definition of national defense to justify the continuation of the project:

> In its broadest sense this education became habilitation and rehabilitation. And as these unskilled people worked day by day, with joy in achievement and in a fundamental [*sic*] became conscious of their growth...—men and women, young and old, white and black, side by side—there came a tolerance for each other with [shared] responsibility for the task to be done.

But funds ran dry and the federal project was shut down in 1943. A similar, though much smaller-scale, county project continued through the 1960s for residents denied employment in the private sector because of advanced age or physical handicap.

With this chapter of Elsa's life concluded, she turned to the summer community of Saugatuck, Michigan, for inspiration. She taught each year at the Summer School of Painting at the Ox Bow Inn and even directed the program for thirteen years, from the late 1940s through the 1950s. The remote rural setting presented artists with picturesque scenes of nature and small-scale fishing, farming, and logging operations. Most important for Elsa, the school was a place where creative minds could mingle and make art without the bureaucracy and formal strictures of art schools that offered degrees.

One such stricture that galled Elsa was her mandatory retirement from the State Teachers' College, at age seventy, in 1955. The *Sentinel* reporter who covered her departure insisted, "Everybody thinks of Miss Ulbricht as young." Fortunately, at Saugatuck, Elsa could continue teaching as long as she was able.

Milwaukee, though, continued to have a hold on Elsa. She still lived in her childhood home; indeed, she shared the space with her mother, Augusta, who lived into her nineties. She continued to teach at the county rehabilitation program, and her students continued to adore her. In the early 1970s, when Elsa herself was approaching ninety, some former students were cleaning her house when they discovered dozens of canvases, hoarded away in corners, some of them even stuck together. It was unanimously determined that a retrospective exhibit of the "artist" Ulbricht—as opposed to the well-known "teacher"—was in order. This pleased Elsa immensely. She had, on occasion, had to apologize to herself for putting students before her own art, which some have estimated to be of considerable merit. A crowd of 750 people thronged the opening, most of all to celebrate her indomitable spirit and express their deeply felt gratitude. Some of the works she exhibited dated back to her New York art school days.

Elsa's final years were spent largely as a local dignitary of Milwaukee. Crafts had been "rediscovered," and a 1970 University of Wisconsin gallery exhibit of the Handicrafts Project reinvigorated Elsa's fame. The economic downturn of the late 1970s caused her to dust off her argument for a permanent "Handicrafts Project." Meanwhile, she fought off physicians who encouraged her to move out of her house to a retirement home. Elsa passed away in 1980 at the age of ninety-five.

EDNA FERBER
1885–1968

Author of the Working Woman

I have decided upon Northwestern University. It has a special program for elocution."

When Edna Ferber, seventeen years old, made this announcement to her parents, she probably expected them to defer to her wishes. After all, she had just won the state high school declamatory contest in Madison, reciting an entire short story from beginning to end and with considerable feeling. The story, by a contemporary author, was about a girl raised in the theater, a world that held a life-long attraction for Edna. Almost all of Appleton, Wisconsin, had turned out for the spontaneous bonfire held on account of her victory. Edna herself had arrived there on the shoulders of Ryan High School football players.

Her family would not hear of it. Evanston, Illinois, was too far away.

Living in a largish house on North Street, they were middle-class but not securely so. Some years earlier, when her father, Jacob, was still in his forties, he had withdrawn from business dealings as his sight began to fail. Somewhat forlornly, he depended upon Edna for

Edna Ferber

company and to rub his forehead when the pain behind his eyes became unbearable. Edna's mother, Julia, supported the family by running their downtown dry-goods store, very capably but with great effort.

The answer, probably spoken by Julia, was a definite "no" to Northwestern.

By her own account, Edna turned on her heels and "in a white hot rage . . . marched down to the office of the *Appleton Daily Crescent*" to ask for a job as the paper's first female reporter. This action, in its fervid independence, is just like something a character in one of Edna's future prize-winning stories, novels, and plays would do. At seventeen, Edna had never anticipated a career as a writer; she fancied herself, instead, as an actress.

Once on "the beat," however, Edna gave great life to Appleton's daily literary fare. Relegated by the editor to features and the Personal and Local items, she vigorously pursued the juiciest bits of gossip the town had to offer. She began her daily rounds with a stop in Ferber's store to discover what interesting transactions her mother might have made, or what inklings the staff of two might have brought from their neighborhoods. Then it was on to Pettibone's Department Store, where the saleswomen often had choice morsels to whisper—while the manager was not looking, of course. Next, perhaps, to the monastery, where, in the shaded courtyard, Edna and Father Basil made a particularly unusual pair of conspirants: he in his brown-corded monk's habit and she in her smart, modern shirtwaist and skirt. Finally, to the courthouse, where she ended each day's rounds, often in a hurry, earning the nickname "Boots" for her tireless bustling after tidbits of news.

Edna opened herself to all kinds of people and experiences. She dined in circus tents with the Fat Lady and the clowns. She talked to farmers and to the gatekeeper at the railroad crossing. When Appleton native Harry Houdini revisited the town, she found him at the drugstore and performed an impromptu interview. No person was too high or too low to be approached by this girl reporter. Appleton, she said, did not encourage such divisions, and she herself never considered them. She spent one and a half years writing newspaper copy. As she wrote later in her autobiography, "The whole community may sift through a reporter's fingers in that time."

What Edna grasped in those years were the telling details by which a person's character and reactions can swiftly be revealed. As a newspaper reporter, Edna developed a penetrating eye for human behavior and social relations, and a disciplined work habit that she never abandoned. This Pulitzer Prize–winning and best-selling author always credited the development of her writing skills to her practical education as a *Crescent* reporter—infinitely more valuable than would have been the formal education she once craved.

* * *

Though born in Kalamazoo, Michigan, Edna's first real memories were of Chicago, where the family lived for a year with her mother's family when Edna was four. The Neumann family originated in Vienna and France, where they engaged in such extravagances as duels, plane-flying, and hunting trips to Africa. The Neumanns then made their way to Wisconsin with the German radical Carl Schurz. As Edna describes them, they were Jewish in their resourcefulness, their restlessness, and their warmhearted, quick-witted "color." Grandpa Neumann worshipped the theater; Grandma mimicked the neighborhood characters. Edna's autobiography, *A Peculiar Treasure*, has much to say about such Jewishness, its strengths and weaknesses and its source in persecution. The book was published in 1939, and reminds its reader in every chapter of the Nazi threat to Jewry—and humanity.

Edna did not know what it meant to be Jewish until the family moved to Ottumwa, a town that needed a shop of the kind Jacob Ferber had opened in Kalamazoo. This large farming and coal-mining town along the Des Moines River in southern Iowa was hardly dull, but hardly pleasant in its rough backwardness. Edna remembered their maids, their curious accents and delicious food, a descent into a mineshaft, the Panic of 1893, the river flooding, Methodist Revival meetings, and the "cross of gold" speech of William Jennings Bryan. But most of all she remembered the little girl down the street and the grown-up idlers at Sargent's Drugstore—the way their eyes always brightened at her approach just for the chance to call someone "sheeny."

Unconsciously, the ever-curious Edna was filing away memories she would use in her later incarnation as an author. More immediately, however, the precocious child was busy demanding her place on the stage. She recited "pieces" incessantly, a practice that had begun in Chicago to an audience of doting grandparents.

It was back to the grandparents that the family retreated when the business in Ottumwa finally collapsed. From there the family's next stop was determined: the small town of Appleton, Wisconsin. Edna was twelve years old—old enough and experienced enough to sense the town's possibilities. In her eyes, Appleton was a miracle of openness and sociability. For starters, the mayor was a Jew. There were forty mostly middle-class Jewish families in town, and no evidence that anyone noticed. The Jewish children at Edna's school were ordinary students, no more singled out for excellence than for abuse. Edna could join any crowd she chose.

At the turn of the century, Appleton was an idyllic Midwestern town. In spring the nearby woods blossomed with wildflowers; in fall they teemed with walnuts and hickory nuts. It was still a formal time, with women wearing corsets and full-length skirts. But children were entitled to be children. In the winter Edna and her friends ice-skated on the frozen Fox River and stole rides on the runners of horse-drawn sleighs. Neighbors socialized. In warmer weather there were picnics beside the river locks and dams.

These locks were the source of much of the town's prosperity. The coursing rapids that had once given the town the name of Grand Chute had been harnessed to power paper mills and other industries. Appleton was a stop on the Chicago Northwestern Railway and had its own streetcar system, along with a hospital, library, and civic center. It was the site of the progressive-minded Lawrence University, the second college in the nation to welcome women students alongside men.

Her later fame and fortune notwithstanding, high school was a high point in Edna's life. In her autobiography she describes her time at Ryan High School, now Appleton Central, as "four miraculous years of the most exhilarating and heartening fun." She dated a succession of boys, performed in school plays, and won local prestige for her dramatic recitals. She credited the school for encouraging independent thought and action.

Edna's school may have encouraged independence, but her mother embodied it. Julia Ferber took over the Ferber Store soon after the family arrived in Appleton due to her husband's failing health. Small-town shopkeeping would not have been her choice in life, but she approached it with aplomb. She made regular solo trips to Chicago and brought back the sensible fashion of the "short" ankle-length skirt, and was the first woman in Appleton to wear it. She found improbable bargains in luxury items and made them sell. Indeed, Julia was a kind of "people person" from whom a future novelist could learn much. All who frequented her shop, from University wives and self-important East Enders to traveling salesmen and broken-down farmwives, eventually confided in her. On occasion, the daughter of Grandma Neumann probably had to stifle her impulse for mimicry. Fascinated, Edna watched this tap-estry of humanity unfold.

The stories that first won Edna Ferber acclaim centered on a traveling petticoat saleswoman named Emma McChesney, and res-onate with the authority of one who knew the business. This charac-ter had all the capability, wit, and dash of Julia Ferber; the fact that she peddled feminine fluffery was a delightful irony. Similarly, Fer-ber's novel *Cimarron* (1929), about Oklahoma, revolves around a small-town newspaper office, much like the one she came to know so well in Appleton.

Edna began writing fiction after her career in journalism came to a careening halt. When a new editor took the helm of the *Crescent*, the local "girl reporter" was driven out. She soon received an offer from the Milwaukee *Journal*, however. With her family's reluctant bless-ing, she moved to a colorful Milwaukee boarding house that became the subject for her first novel, *Dawn O'Hara*. Though she loved writ-ing for the newspaper—tagging "Fighting Bob" La Follette for an interview or getting the scoop on the plundering of Wisconsin's forests (fodder for her later novel, *Come and Get It*)—the relentless pressures of the job eventually wore her out. One morning while dressing for work she fainted in her room.

Edna returned to Appleton and virtually collapsed with anemia. One day several months later she staggered home with a used type-writer and set it up in a corner of the family house. Her first work was a response to a contest calling for essays on "How I Lost My Job." Edna won the contest. Then, she purchased a ream of yellow paper and sat down to type *Dawn O'Hara*, a novel about an attractive Milwaukee newspaperwoman married to the wrong man. One year later, she had finished. Edna's rebirth as a fiction writer was as abrupt and instinctive as that.

Foremost in Edna's mind was her need for a solid income. When

Dawn O'Hara was rejected and returned by three different women's magazines, she put it away and began a short story, "The Homely Heroine." In the midst of this effort, her long-ailing father Jacob died. Anxious to be rid of the store, Julia began planning the family's move back to Chicago. Edna literally finished her story between packing boxes, sent it off to a magazine, and heard that it was accepted. She finished another successful story just before she, Julia, and sister Fanny moved to Chicago. In the final stages of cleaning out the house, Edna found *Dawn O'Hara*. Instead of feeding it to the coal-burning furnace along with her other drafts, she packaged and sent it to a woman agent whom she'd overheard Zona Gale—the first of Wisconsin's famous female authors—recommend. Within months of the family's arrival in Chicago, the novel was accepted. Edna began to believe in that most unexpected possibility, a career as a fiction writer.

For the next couple of years, Edna lived an itinerant life centered mostly at the family's South-Side flat in Chicago but in New York and European hotels as well. She churned out text in the morning and took in her surroundings in the afternoons. Once she had opened the Emma McChesney vein, journals clamored for her work. From 1910 to 1916, Edna mined the short story market, becoming a regular contributor to mainstream publications. In 1912 she won the assignment of feature "women's" correspondent for the Democratic and Republican national conventions—before women could even vote! She began finding people with whom her intellect "clicked." Early in 1914 she sailed to Europe for an extended six-month tour. Alone and independent, she changed venues and accepted invitations as she wished, all the while maintaining her daily writing regimen on rented typewriters. She returned just as World War I had begun.

Once the United States entered the war, Edna fervidly lent her services writing propaganda for the Red Cross and Salvation Army and giving speeches across the nation encouraging the war effort. Looking back to this time in her 1939 biography, she called the so-called "Great War" a "holocaust"—a word that took on new dimensions in later years. The war's effects on the American public were, in fact, numbing. In covering the 1920 Republican convention, Edna described Warren G. Harding as having the look of a model statesman, "until you looked in his eyes. . . . There was nothing behind them." When World War II arrived, Edna again felt drawn to public service and public comment, this time more intensely. In 1945 she succeeded in gaining entry to Germany as a V.I.P. war correspondent. Back home, in speeches for War Bonds, she raged about the effects of appeasement and the fate of Jews.

The only other political cause Edna embraced in her life was that of Adlai Stevenson, the Illinois Democrat who ran for president against Dwight D. Eisenhower in 1952 and 1956. She appreciated his uncommonly sharp mind and honest speech and stumped for him on several occasions. Earlier in his career Stevenson had spoken out against the "Red Scare" legislation limiting the civil rights of Americans—legislation sponsored, incidentally, by an Appleton native, Senator Joe McCarthy.

Almost all of Edna's novels have a sociological interest, often with a sentimental bent for the "little guy." They are based on glimpses of real life or of real people the author saw and then nurtured in her imagination. For some novels, such as *Ice Palace*, set in Alaska, her research involved adventure; others began with ideas she simply could not escape. She set her novels in vastly diverse milieus, from Texas oil fields, newly settled Oklahoma, and the lumberjack world of Michigan forests to the New York commercial district and turn-of-the century New Orleans Creole culture. Indeed, her novels traverse much of the great American landscape. One U.S. serviceman wrote Edna a letter from England to say her writing had cheered him and the boys by reminding them of their homeland.

Her best novels reveal her fascination with that new American phenomenon, the working woman. Surely Edna, with her disciplined approach to writing and publishing, identified with these heroines. Edna's accomplishment in single-handedly maintaining her relatively lavish New York City lifestyle, as well as supporting her ailing mother, who herself had supported a family on her own, must have been a most vivid reality for her.

One seed for a novel came to Edna in a 1919 Chicago produce market, when she glimpsed a single woman vendor among the sea of men dealing vegetables from their carts. The displaced farmers she saw in Chicago, those who had sold their land but never acclimated to city life, had been long on her mind. She began to imagine a woman whose attitude toward the land combined the strength of the farmers she'd known in Appleton with the exuberance of Emma McChesney—a woman who lived in the masculine world of farming and commerce, but did so with feminine grace. Thus was born the character of Selina DeJong and Edna's first best-seller, *So Big* (1924), which sold 323,000 copies, won the Pulitzer Prize, and made her one of America's best-loved authors of the time. Edna did not intend to write a best-seller and believed that no novel about the beauty of cabbages could possibly sell. Having read the manuscript, though, her publishers told her otherwise. *So Big* was in one sense an American "take" on the Victorian novelistic convention that "virtue wins out in the end," or "the cream rises to the top." For in the case of Selina, "the top" was self-satisfaction in life. That Selina began this "climb" only after being widowed, and achieved such heights on an Illinois truck farm was incredibly refreshing, if not revolutionary. Selina's creative life in the dirt is contrasted to her son's timid life in the business career that her sweat and enterprise enabled. The novel was both nostalgic in its romancing of the land and forward-looking in its feminism.

Contrasting a strong woman character with weak and dispensable male characters became a pattern in Edna's books for which she was ultimately criticized. One reader responding to a review of *Giant*, her best-selling novel satirizing the oil-rich braggadocio, racism, and parochialism of Texas, explained that Edna simply did not like the state because it was not sufficiently "womaned":

> By this time the warped thinking of Miss Ferber on the feebleness of the male animal should be obvious. Her books retread the same ground to a degree that even a casual reader can predict the outcome in advance. . . . Only the women are worth their salt! It is obvious that Miss Ferber's contention is that men may be attractive, but only in the sense that children are attractive. She seems to feel men are only excess baggage in her tidy little feministic world. Thus in her books, without exception, women are the builders, men are picturesque—but really useless.

He was not the only reader to make this conclusion. In this light, it's even more remarkable that Ferber's work was as widely read as it was. Her worst flaw may have been her most significant contribution.

In life, Ferber preferred the company of men to women; with men, she was free to exercise her intellect freely and with the acid authority it naturally commanded. She felt comfortable as a woman in a man's world, as when doing the gritty reporting of the national party conventions. In other settings she became self-conscious about her appearance, which she frequently deprecated, even after regular visits to the beauty salon, and one trip to a plastic surgeon for a nose job. She remained, throughout life, "Miss Ferber," despite the existence of suitors. Edna simply chose to be single; her parents' mismatched marriage and her own fear of "being bored" with domesticity weighed heavily in this decision.

Edna's home was ultimately New York City, the home of Broadway and publishers alike. She engaged in numerous dramatic collaborations with the playwright George Kauffman and one with Oscar Hammerstein for a musical rendition of her novel set on the great Mississippi, *Show Boat*. In the Depression of the 1930s, her novels and plays became hot movie properties, with the film releases of *Cimarron* (1930), starring Irene Dunne; *So Big* (1932), starring Barbara Stanwyck; *Dinner at 8* (1933), starring Marie Dressler; *Show Boat* (1936), starring Dunne and including a performance by Paul Robeson; *Come and Get It* (1936), starring Frances Farmer; and *Stage Door* (1937), starring Katharine Hepburn and Ginger Rogers. The 1950s saw the release of another version of *Show Boat* (1951), starring Kathryn Grayson and Ava Gardner, and *Giant* (1956), with its superstar cast of Liz Taylor, Rock Hudson, and James Dean. The contacts she had with producers, directors, and actors began to define her life; she frequently entertained her showbiz friends at her apartment.

As Ferber's wealth increased, she was extravagantly generous to those she loved, both friends and family. On a walk through downtown Manhattan, a friend who remarked to Edna about an item in a store window might find that item on her doorstep the very next day. Such gestures also suggest Edna's need for attention, a weakness that grew worse with age. As the quality of her work declined late in life, she became desperate for praise and refused to accept even constructive criticism; she had become a bit spoiled by her fame. But one can forgive a crotchety old woman her vanities. Edna Ferber invented dozens of female characters that enabled the women of her day to see themselves in a new, enabling light. These characters might dress stylishly—as Edna did—but they were primarily heroines of action and intelligence, independent of men. The main heroine was always herself, and the best of her works is her spirited autobiography, *A Peculiar Treasure*. That so public a woman could write so frankly at that time about her Jewishness seems terribly courageous, though of course one wishes it didn't.

Edna died in 1968 after a two-year battle with cancer.

MABEL WATSON RAIMEY
1898–1986

In Defense of Dignity

*I*t was Mabel Raimey's third day teaching elementary school in the Milwaukee Public School System. She was experiencing the excitement that comes with one's first job. She already adored the young students in her charge. She was barely twenty.

With only isolated facts of this event on record, we are left to imagine the scene upon her arrival that day. Mabel, wearing the full skirts of the time, bustled past the front office. Perhaps she sensed the furtive glances cast her way, or the unusual quiet when she entered a room. Unbeknownst to her, gossip about her had been spreading quickly around the school that morning.

A school administrator stopped her. "May I have a word with you, Miss Raimey?"

Trained in English literature, she knew the proper words to say in response to his request, and spoke them with proper dignity.

Indeed, she was certain: People were staring at her.

The principal closed the door to his office and sat behind his desk. "Miss Raimey, it has come to my attention that. . . . " Perhaps he stopped, mid-sentence. Perhaps some part of him found it difficult to utter the prejudice he held.

Mabel Watson Raimey

"Sir?" young Mabel would have encouraged him.

"Miss Raimey, might you apprise me of your ancestral race?"

Mabel could do so, had she wished. Her great-great-grand-mother Molly was the daughter of a chief in Guinea. Molly and her brother had been lured aboard a slave ship by the promise of an education in the New World. The Virginia slaveowner who bene-fited from this cruelty fathered Molly's son, Sully, who later arrived in Milwaukee as a freed slave. He brought with him his wife, Susan, a second-generation freeborn African American. Mabel had seen their tintype images, more than once. But Mabel doubted that this principal cared to know all that. What he wanted to know was her *race*. She stammered and blushed: "Sir?" she repeated.

The man behind the desk grinned. "Let me put it in simple terms for you. Are—you—a—Negro?"

Mabel caught her breath. "Yes, I am sir, but I don't see . . . ."

As the man began to speak, Mabel must have heard only his tone. Feigned apology at what he "must" do. Amusement. Conde-scension. Her body turned cold. Mabel held her head high as she turned to leave his office. Then, striding toward the door, she heard the secretary giggle. She whirled. Behind her, the principal's expres-sion was that of a child caught in mischief. He had been making faces at her for the amusement of his staff.

The event changed Mabel's life. Fifty years later, she still remembered the expression on that man's face.

* * *

Mabel's ancestors were among Milwaukee's first African-American residents. Rather than merely "tolerated," they were respected members of the community. In the mid-nineteenth century, Wisconsin was an abolitionist, Republican stronghold. The state was proud of its participation in the Union cause. In

Milwaukee some 200 blacks worked and lived side-by-side with whites, some holding jobs as skilled laborers and residing in middle-class neighborhoods. Many of the early African-American residents were "mulattos" of dual ancestry, like Mabel and her family.

This proud heritage had begun to fade by the time of Mabel's birth. The abuses and violence of the post–Reconstruction era in the South seemed to invigorate racism across the nation. As the urban economy evolved from a commercial to an industrial one, it was the new European immigrants, not the blacks, who won the factory jobs. African Americans were relegated to menial jobs, serving as cooks, porters, waiters, and the like. If they were given jobs in factories, it was in the role of strikebreakers. Black workers were not part of the burgeoning union movement: The unions excluded them. This "scab" role greatly increased tensions between the races.

Still, as Mabel grew up, her mother, Nellie Raimey, could point to certain homes and public buildings—the Iron Block Building, the Soldier's Home, the second Milwaukee County Courthouse—and tell her, "Your grand-daddy Watson built those." William Thomas Watson, Sully's eldest son, was a skilled mason in Milwaukee during the 1850s and 1860s. A daguerreotype now housed in the Milwaukee Public Museum's collection shows a strikingly handsome man, wearing a fashionable suit and collar. This image was among the family's proud possessions.

Mabel's own father, Anthony Raimey, was a mail clerk. Anthony and Nellie lived on Walnut Street in an area that was gradually becoming the "Black District," but was also home to thousands of Jewish immigrants. The Raimeys took great pride in their only child's academic accomplishments, saving mementos from her earliest years at school. Mabel graduated from West Division High School at the precocious age of fourteen. She received training in education at Milwaukee Normal School, then attended

the University of Wisconsin at Madison, earning a four-year bac-
calaureate degree in English. It is believed she was the first African-
American woman to graduate from that institution, although there
may have been others with similarly light skin tone who never let
their secret be known.

It is not surprising that Mabel was shocked at her treatment
by the principal of the elementary school where she went to teach.
With her accomplishments, her youth, and her family's pride, she
must have felt a touch of invincibility. It was not that she hadn't
met previous obstacles: Her family physician had discouraged her
from medicine because "women couldn't handle the studies." But
she had certainly proven herself academically. She had lived up to
her own high standards. And she had not been derailed by people
who were content to keep their standards low.

After such a rude awakening, what could an educated young
woman of high standards do? In 1919 Mabel volunteered her services to the newly founded Milwaukee Chapter of the National
Urban League. The mission of this "educational social work
agency" was to promote interracial cooperation through speaking
engagements, radio spots, and integrated social functions, while at
the same time providing much-needed recreational opportunities,
job training, and health services to local black communities. It was
a remarkable achievement for the twenty-one-year-old Mabel to
transform her shock and anger into wholehearted efforts address-
ing the root cause of the cruelty she had endured.

After she lost her teaching job, Mabel began working as a ste-
nographer for a lawyer in the First Wisconsin National Bank
Building downtown. After a few years of this work, she enrolled at
Marquette University Law School and began attending evening
classes while continuing to work by day. She knew that she was the
first African-American woman to attend the law school, but
nobody asked about her "ancestral race," nor did she volunteer the

information. In the common lingo, she "passed." And in 1927, she also passed the state bar exam, becoming the first black woman lawyer in Wisconsin. Vel Phillips, the second black woman to join the Wisconsin bar, would not do so until 1951.

After graduation Mabel continued to work for the lawyer at the bank building as a legal secretary. Only when he died did she venture out on her own. She took on clients "regardless of their race, color, creed, or economic ability," attempting to perform her services "in a fair and just manner." From the 1930s through the 1940s, she was one of only three African-American lawyers in the city. Yet many of her clients were white—mostly friends and acquaintances from the Tabernacle Baptist Church she regularly attended. Mabel was active in this fully integrated church through-out her life, and was known to don overalls to check the furnace, and make strong coffee for meetings, as well as provide legal advice in her role as trustee.

At the Milwaukee Urban League, Mabel advanced from vol-unteer secretary to full-fledged member of the board, which included other black professionals and prominent white employers, along with social workers. She also founded the Milwaukee branch of the Alpha Kappa Alpha sorority, a service organization prima-rily for African-American women. And, because the YWCA at the time denied membership to black women, she helped establish a branch of the YWCA for the black community, later renamed Vel Phillips Center.

Despite her commitment and service to African Americans, her readiness to associate with whites caused suspicion and even dis-like within the increasingly class- and race-conscious black commu-nity. This dislike was symptomatic of a growing class rift among Milwaukee blacks. In the late twenties, an African-American edito-rialist with working-class sympathies described the more established black community in Milwaukee as "a bunch of self-chosen 'exclu-sives' " who complained about discrimination but did nothing to contribute to black institutions. In such a climate it would not be surprising if Mabel experienced a kind of "reverse discrimination." And, it is true that the Milwaukee Urban League had, as part of its early "educational" efforts, pressed the point with whites that not all "Negroes" were the same, that some had middle-class ambition and drive and, presumably, weren't like "those others."

Mabel must have been aware of this ferment, but she chose not to concern herself with the talk. One Milwaukee resident painted the impression she, as a child, had of Mabel crossing the downtown bridge: "stoic, beautiful, walking with her head held high, looking neither left nor right." Later, Mabel would encourage young audiences to set high goals and "never use sex or race as an excuse not to attain these goals." To change her course because some did not approve of it would have been unthinkable to her.

Still, there is something melancholy in her story. After her mother, Nellie, died, Mabel lived alone. Her status was a conscious choice. Over the years she had received three marriage offers but rejected them in favor of her career; in those days, women did not combine the two. When she was asked in the 1980s whether mar-ried women should have a career, ever the traditionalist, she rejected the idea.

The home she returned to each evening was the same Walnut Street house in which she was raised, full of antiques belonging to the family. Advancing through her forties and fifties, she saw her neighborhood deteriorate. As Milwaukee's African-American pop-ulation grew from 12,000 in 1940 to about 70,000 in the early 1960s, this area rapidly became the crowded "Inner Core" of the black ghetto. Politically minded blacks saw racial injustice as being at the root of this problem. The practice of restricting blacks to just a few older neighborhoods, combined with unrealistic rents, caused families to double up, which in turn hastened structural and social deterioration.

All along, the approach of the Urban League had been to help African-American newcomers in practical ways. After a point it became clear that the most practical step toward improving the lot of the black community was through political means—through an insistence on civil rights. Into this fray stepped Vel Phillips, representative of an entirely different generation. In 1956 Vel was elected to the Milwaukee Common Council. In 1962 she introduced a law that would prohibit discrimination in housing based on race. After dozens of marches, rallies, and protests, this law finally was enacted in 1968. Vel commented, "The council has given me hope. Maybe the white power structure recognizes the frustrations of the black community." Mabel would never have spoken these words. The reform movement had passed her by.

Then, in 1972—four years after this turning-point in Milwaukee's black history—Mabel experienced a second turning-point of her own. Mabel was taking a bath one day when she experienced numbness, dizziness, and confusion—the typical signs of a stroke. Mabel lost consciousness; when she awoke, she found that she could not move one entire side of her body. She tried, but could not get out of the bathtub. Mabel stayed in the bathtub for five days before a concerned friend discovered her there. She later explained how she had survived by drinking her bathwater.

After this nightmare episode, Mabel was confined to a wheelchair and forced to move to a retirement home. She could no longer practice law. In many respects she faded from sight, except for her continuing attendance at the Tabernacle Baptist Church. There, she gravitated to the youngsters, seeking to mentor them into adulthood. In retrospect, they remembered her kindness, dignity, and wisdom. Despite her bodily impediments and her impaired speech, she remained a commanding presence at the church.

When Mabel reached the end of her life, the public began to honor her accomplishments and recognize her contributions. In 1984 the Milwaukee chapter of the National Association of Black Women Attorneys was named after her. The same year the University of Wisconsin Alumni Association presented her the Scroll of Excellence. Mabel accepted these awards with humility:

> If my acceptance and completion of law school at Marquette University in the 1920s has inspired or encouraged anyone to enter the field of law, I am pleased. If any accomplishment that I may have made has had any influence on any young people, I am pleased more.

Mabel died at the age of eighty-five, from complications of pneumonia. A state historical marker with her name and remarkable story now stands at Marquette University Law School.

GOLDA MEIR
1898–1978

Prime Minister of Israel

$\mathcal{G}$olda Meir, seventy years old, enjoyed being a grand-mother. The former foreign minister of the new state of Israel had just left decades of public service behind to join the citizenry of Israel. In her own words, she "felt like a prisoner released from jail." She found herself taking "enormous pleasure" in the most ordinary daily tasks of shopping, cooking, cleaning, ironing, reading books—and, of course, visiting her grandchildren.

Then, late in February 1969, she received the news. Israel's prime minister, Levi Eshkol, her friend and fellow Labor Party member, had died. Before he had even been buried, newspaper reporters were asking, who else but Golda would become the next prime minister of Israel?

This was not how she had envisioned her retirement. In 1967 Israel waged and won the Six Day War against its Arab neighbors; although the decisive victory had expanded Isreal's territory, it had not given the nation peace. Every week brought reports of more Israelis killed by Egyptians, Syrians, Lebanese, Jordanians, and Palestinians. Another war was imminent. Becoming prime minister

Golda Meir

would mean waking up in the morning—and sometimes in the middle of the night—with this threat to Israel's existence foremost in her mind.

Nonetheless, when the Labor Party convened to nominate its interim minister, Golda received 100 percent of the votes. She sat in the chamber, tears rolling down her cheeks. As she explained in her autobiography, "I only knew that now I would have to make decisions every day that would affect the lives of millions of people." She went on to serve Israel as prime minister for four years.

Golda had cried in public before. She had been part of the solemnities on May 14, 1948, the day that Israel declared its statehood. On that day, 2,000 years of Jewish homelessness came to an end. In the Tel Aviv Museum, as she signed the proclamation, she thought of all who had given their lives in order for this moment to occur.

She thought nothing of the sacrifices she herself had made.

✶ ✶ ✶

Golda Mabovich was born in Kiev, Ukraine, in 1898, during the reign of Czar Nicholas II. Kiev was "off-limits" to Jews, but Golda's father had received special permission to move there because of his talent as a carpenter. This official dispensation proved a curse, as anti-Semitism kept him unemployed and made the family and their small community subject to death raids— pogroms—by hate groups armed with knives and sticks. The memory of her father nailing a few planks across their windows to defend the family stayed with Golda the rest of her years. This kind of powerlessness, she felt, no people should have to endure.

Golda was five when her father immigrated to the United States in search of a job; she and her two sisters moved with her mother to Pinsk. Pinsk was part of the Pale, a region in Belarus where Jews were allowed to settle. In such a place Jewish cultural life and political ideas thrived. But even Jews in Pinsk could not be free from the fear of pogroms: Sword-wielding Cossacks, the free-wheeling paramilitary of the czars, had been at war with the Jews for centuries and could sweep through on horseback at any time.

In Pinsk, Golda's older sister Sheyna soon became involved in a group promoting Theodor Herzl's idea of a Jewish state. This idea, known as Zionism, was often combined with socialist economic ideas; the debate raged in Pinsk about whether socialism or Zionism should come first. Fourteen-year-old Sheyna and her co-conspirators held impassioned political meetings in the family's kitchen when her mother was not there. Golda would hide in a niche above the stove, listening in fascination to their discussions about how to overthrow the czar and create a socialist Jewish state in Palestine.

It wasn't long before Golda's mother began to fear for Sheyna's safety. Deliverance from these worries eventually came in a letter from her husband, who was then in Milwaukee. He had finally gotten a job working on the railway. It was time for the family to reunite. In 1906 Golda and her family traveled in the steerage class of an ocean liner, hardly able to imagine what would greet them on the other side.

Young Golda was bewildered by Milwaukee. There was the incredible pace of an American industrial city. There was the English language spoken all around her. There was her father, looking changed from how she remembered him. And there was his insistence that they abandon their "peasant" skirts and blouses for more modern, American garb. Not to mention the cars! She had never ridden in one before.

Golda and her mother both adapted marvelously. Within two weeks, her mother was running a store on Walnut Street (not far from where Mabel Raimey was growing up), and Golda was attending school on Fourth Street, next to the Schlitz brewery. Their two commitments often conflicted. To stock the store, Golda's mother rose early for the wholesale market in the center of town, leaving her daughter in charge of the store. When she was delayed, Golda would be marooned in the shop after the school day had begun. She loved school and hated being tardy and grew to loathe her shop duty.

Otherwise, Golda thrived. She was not the only girl who came to school knowing only Yiddish; she lived in a section of town populated largely by European Jewish immigrants. Being young, she learned English easily. She formed close friendships and soaked up the learning her teachers offered.

There had been no public schools in Pinsk. Here, in America, education was free, though students had to pay textbook user fees. When she was eleven years old and in fourth grade, Golda noticed that many of the children in her school could not afford to pay these fees, and thus went without textbooks. As if it were her second nature, Golda organized her first fundraising event. She and a friend, Regina Hamburger, and some other girls formed the "American Young Sisters Society." They rented a meeting hall and sent out invitations to the entire school district. Dozens showed up for Golda's unrehearsed speech about the need of all children for textbooks. All the money that was needed was raised. The event received coverage in the local newspaper, and Golda received much praise from her family and neighbors.

Golda had learned what was possible in America. She had also come to know what it meant to live without fear. An incident at a Labor Day parade brought this message home. Labor Day was a holiday for which Milwaukee, a workers' town, "pulled out all of the stops," including a parade led by the city's mounted policemen. Standing on the street corner with the rest of the family, Golda's younger sister saw the officers on horseback and screamed, "The

Cossacks! The Cossacks are coming!" Her sister's outburst caused Golda to reflect on the fact that she and her family were now safer than they had ever been. Later, she would comment that she never once encountered anti-Semitism in Milwaukee.

Upon graduating from the lower grades as class valedictorian, Golda made a shocking discovery. Her parents, who had supported her academic achievements up to this point, did not wish for her to attend high school. Indeed, they would not allow it. Golda's ambition was to become a schoolteacher. Her parents' version of her future was to find a promising young man to marry, and attend secretarial school only if necessary. Her father told her, "Men don't like smart girls."

Golda's older sister, Sheyna, the "revolutionary," had moved to Denver years earlier. There she lived with her fiancé, Shamai, who had followed her from Pinsk. Golda wrote of the family quarrel in her letters to Sheyna, whose letters in turn encouraged her to keep fighting for her education. And fight she did: Golda defied her parents' wishes and began attending high school. This "victory" increased the acrimony at home, which was becoming too much for Golda to bear. Sheyna finally invited Golda to live with her in Denver. They would have to struggle to survive, but at least Golda could pursue her education in peace. One morning, instead of going to school, Golda left the house, picked up a bundle of clothes at her friend Regina's house, and headed for the train station.

In Denver, Sheyna's home attracted young Yiddish-speaking intellectuals and socialists for informal evening chats. In a reprise of her Pinsk childhood, Golda would listen from a kitchen nook as visitors discussed subjects ranging from the philosophy of Shopenhauer to the benefits of an eight-hour workday, frequently touching on the Zionist experiment of the first Jewish settlers in Palestine. Golda developed a fondness for Morris Meyerson, a bespectacled sign painter who gladly supplemented her neglected high school coursework with private lectures on history and poetry and trips to the symphony. When, three years later, Golda received a letter calling her home, Morris confessed his love. She returned to Milwaukee secure with the promise of future marriage.

In the three years she had been gone, her parents had become pillars of the Milwaukee Jewish community, hosting visiting speakers at their home and serving on various committees to aid the Jewish Legions fighting in World War I. Many of the visitors were members of the *yishuv*, the small Jewish community living in Palestine. Their talk whetted her appetite for the same kind of adventure and achievement. After all, what sense was there in being a Zionist if one were not also a pioneer?

In 1917 Golda organized a march in downtown Milwaukee protesting the treatment of Jews in Poland and the Ukraine. Although it was a success, drawing Jews and gentiles alike, it nonetheless led her to an epiphany: There was a world of difference between symbolic action and real action, and Golda knew to which camp she belonged.

She wrote to Morris, stating that she wanted both to marry him and to go to Palestine. Essentially, she gave him no choice. He was finally swayed when, in November 1917, Great Britain issued the Balfour Declaration, favoring "the establishment in Palestine of a National Home for the Jewish People." (Britain had acquired Palestine when the Ottoman Empire collapsed.) One month later the couple was married in the Mabovich home. Their marriage in no way impeded Golda's activities; much to her father's chagrin, she traveled on behalf of the Labor Zionists to Chicago, New York, Canada, and Philadelphia. Finally, in 1920, word came of openings on the SS *Pocahontas*, setting out for Palestine from New York Harbor. Golda and Morris said their good-byes to family and friends, in the process recruiting Sheyna and Shamai to join them.

In May 1921, the *Pocahontas* set sail. The only extravagance the Meyersons brought with them was their wind-up phonograph.

Golda would return to the United States many times, but never to stay. In the community that later became Israel, she would often boast of Milwaukee as her home, perhaps because everyone associated Milwaukee with organized labor, one of the chief values held by the young socialist society gathering in clusters in the desert. For years Golda held prominent positions in the Histradut, the state's labor organization. Of course, the concerns of Histradut were not the same as those of labor unions in the industrial world back home; in Palestine, "labor" then consisted of a few scattered enterprises and groups of hopeful pioneers living on kibbutzim.

It was Golda's intention to join a kibbutz immediately upon arriving. These small agricultural societies were arranged communally so that men and women worked together for the common good. Many were formed on formerly untillable ground, the first task being to drain or irrigate the land to make it suitable for cultivation. Once they arrived in Palestine, though, she and Morris found it difficult to gain entry into Merhavia, the kibbutz of their choice. Golda and Morris simply appeared too refined to accept the deprivation of primitive agricultural life. They were finally admitted, Golda would later joke, merely because of their phonograph.

The commune's assessment of Morris may have been accurate. But, given the chance, Golda threw herself into the work. She surprised the women by volunteering to cook—a job they looked down on as "women's work"—and then by adding touches of beauty and taste to their meager repasts. Life on the kibbutz suited her. She liked to knead bread. She enjoyed staying up late chatting with the guards. She went on to become the kibbutz expert on raising poultry and was voted onto the kibbutz's steering committee. This duty took her to a conference in Degania, where she rubbed elbows with many of the men who had so impressed her on their tours through Milwaukee.

This inspiring memory would have to last Golda awhile, for she and Morris soon left Merhavia at his insistence. He could not tolerate its intense ideology and lack of privacy; for him, these seemed to squelch the very poetry out of life. Furthermore, he wanted to raise his own children. Golda tore herself away from what for her was the core Zionist experience and moved with her husband to Jerusalem and the four "most miserable" years of her life.

Golda's discontent stemmed from the isolation of remaining home with first one, and then two, infants. This, coupled with the limitations of poverty, shrank her world to the boundaries of her four walls. Jerusalem itself, the most historic city in the world, failed to impress her. In fact, had she noticed it, she might have felt even more painfully that she had been sidetracked from her vision.

In 1927, she began to take solo trips to Tel Aviv, where her sister and now her parents lived. In 1928 she landed a job in that city coordinating the women's council of Histradut, and moved there with her two children, Menachim and Sarah. Full marital separation from Morris would not come for another ten years. Her fluency in English quickly earned her notice. When she spoke at a 1930 Labor Conference in London, her eloquence was noticed by David Ben-Gurion, one of the driving political forces behind an independent Israel. From then on, Golda's stature with her people only increased.

In the period after World War I, Britain back-peddled on the promises it had made to the Jews in Palestine. Arabs were responding with violence to the encroachment of Jews upon their land. Britain had not reckoned on any of this and opted for the path of least resistance: supporting the Arabs, who vastly outnumbered the Jews. With no one else to protect them, Jews in Palestine started their own underground military, the Haganah. Golda Meyerson was among the first to join.

The situation was worse for Jews elsewhere. In 1933 Hitler became chancellor of Germany. The next year, Golda was appointed to the Histradut's executive committee. Her philosophy of labor was well defined by that point. For Golda, people were not tools and labor was not a commodity: "Even for the best purposes, it is a crime to turn an individual into simply a means for an ultimate end. A society in which the dignity of the individual is destroyed cannot hope to be a decent society." Hitler's persecution of Jews presented Golda with a difficult problem: the immigration to Palestine of 70,000 refugees, ranging in skills from the professional classes to the illiterate. Unemployment swelled. It was Golda's job to convince those who were employed at living wages to contribute to an unemployment fund for those who were not. As always, Golda appealed to the enlightened "common good" to get her way. Meanwhile, the enraged Arab Palestinians rioted and petitioned Britain to end Jewish immigration and encroachment on their lands. The White Paper of 1939 did just that, barring Jewish immigration beyond 75,000 and prohibiting Jews from purchasing land. Soon, as Britain became drawn into Hitler's war, the arguing ceased.

After the war, ships full of Jews released from Hitler's concentration camps arrived near the shores of Palestine, their dream of safe haven from the horrors they had left. To everyone's shock, including Golda's, a British blockade forced them to turn back. This injustice tore at Golda's heart and infuriated her at the same time. Such British intransigence is what drew her further into the Haganah during the war years. At one point she even stood trial for Haganah's theft of British munitions. In 1946 anguish for those on board led her to declare a hunger strike in solidarity. As a result, 1,000 refugees received safe harbor.

Finally, in 1947, Britain turned over the problem of Palestine to the fledgling United Nations. As she would in many subsequent trips, Golda raised millions of dollars in America to help pay for the battle that was sure to follow any declaration made by the Special Committee on Palestine. The committee decided that Israel would be a partitioned state, beginning May 14, 1948. The battles Israel fought with its Arab neighbors between then and 1969 were never-ending. As fiercely as Golda committed herself to these territorial battles, she never forgot the ideals that had drawn her to the *yishuv* in the first place. Throughout her long tenure as Israel's labor minister, she drew attention to the problems of the poor in her country and continually appealed to Israelis to help their destitute brothers and sisters; she demanded that the economic system absorb these people.

Golda also reached out to the poor in other nations. When, in 1956, she became Israel's foreign minister and claimed the Hebraic name "Meir," she turned her eyes to Africa. From then until 1966, Golda Meir promoted the sharing of Israeli expertise in such fields as agriculture and health with the emerging African nations. Cynics saw this effort as designed to gain Israel votes in the United Nations assemblies. Even if that were true, however, helping others without indebting them financially is a more enlightened form of persuasion than threats or bribes. Golda certainly felt more than exigency; she identified the raw hope on the African faces she saw with the hope of the Jews arriving in Palestine, and felt "the bond of brotherhood and shared aspirations."

It is perhaps this capacity for human sharing that marks Golda as not just remarkable but great. Though she was passionate about serving Israel, she was never single-minded. This same humanity can be seen in the anecdote of her 1971 return as prime minister to the very school in Milwaukee she had attended as a girl. The faces on the children had changed from Jewish to African-American, but the expression on those faces had not. According to Golda Meir's autobiography, *My Life*, she decided to speak to these students not about book learning but about something more personal:

> "It isn't really important to decide when you are very young just exactly what you want to become when you grow up," I told them. "It is much more important to decide on the way you want to live. If you are going to be honest with yourself and honest with your friends, if you are going to get involved with causes which are good for others, not only for yourselves, then it seems to me that that is sufficient, and maybe what you will be is only a matter of chance." I had a feeling that they understood me.

Two years later, in 1973, Golda would face the horror of a full-scale assault on her country while she was its leader. After months and years of diplomacy in which Israel had misunderstood the gravity of Egypt's threats, Syria and Egypt, backed by nine Arab nations, launched a coordinated attack on Yom Kippur, the holiest day of the Jewish calendar. The Jews repelled the invaders beyond their borders before the United Nations called a cease-fire, but the war was a terrible blow to Golda. Though she was re-elected late in 1973, she resigned in 1974, saying to herself and her friends in the party, "There is a limit to what I can do, and I have now reached that limit."

Would that we all have such broad horizons. Golda Meir died in 1978 and was buried on Mount Herzl in Jerusalem.

MILDRED FISH-HARNACK
1902–1943

Hitler's Scapegoat

*L*ook, darling. An elk!"

Mildred and her husband gazed in amazement at the creature through the pine trees. It was large and powerful, and so close they could see its muscular chest fill with air. At that moment, as they too inhaled the salty air from the Baltic Ocean, breathing must have seemed a gift, nature a startling reality. The wild animal in its natural setting was a lifetime away from the couple's troubles in Berlin. It was the summer of 1942, and Mildred and Arvid were deeply involved in an espionage ring intent on bringing down Hitler's Third Reich.

The following day they were joined on their holiday by a couple the Harnacks knew from Berlin's Marburg University, where Mildred taught literature. Together they had rented a quaint fisherman's cottage halfway up the Curonian spit, at Preil, in present-day Lithuania, a country then occupied by the Germans. It was a surreal setting for the events of the next morning: Arvid coming in from outdoors, followed by three well-dressed men; Arvid telling Mildred to pack for their return to Berlin. To Mildred, who had lived for years in dread of

Mildred Fish-Harnack

this very moment, there was no need to explain. When her friends brought coffee for the men, whom they assumed were visitors, Mildred collapsed in tears at the table. Shakily, she rose to finish packing and made the bed, taking refuge in routine.

The men were members of the Gestapo, Adolf Hitler's dreaded secret police. The Harnack circle, dubbed the "Red Orchestra" because their transmitters were code-named after musical instruments, had been fatally compromised. Mildred and her husband were taken directly to Gestapo headquarters in Berlin, where they were imprisoned in narrow, solitary cells along with other members of the spy ring. Mildred was allowed no visitors; she was deprived food and water for a time, then interrogated.

It was a strange predicament for a girl from Wisconsin. In fact Mildred would become the only American civilian executed by the Gestapo. As the chill of winter edged closer to her cell in the basement of Prince-Albrecht-Strasse 8, she had time to examine the forty years of her life, and to experience the full extent of her despair.

* * *

Mildred Fish was born in Milwaukee in 1902, a late addition to a family of six. Her father, William Fish, was a well-born ne'er-do-well, while her mother, Georgina, studied the texts and doctrines of Christian Science. The family suffered both from William's lackluster work habits and the economic depression of the early 1900s. Mildred's mother took menial jobs to try to make up the difference, but the family was forced to move to successively more run-down dwellings. Growing up, Mildred knew the shame and deprivation of the lower classes. At the same time, she absorbed the grace of her patient, sacrificing—yet determined—mother.

William and Georgina were in the process of separating when World War I broke out. Mildred was twelve, just beginning to dream of being a writer. Emotionally, she joined the public frenzy, writing patriotic poems and a juvenile story of wartime love, "Mein Kamerad," for her school's literary magazine. Meanwhile, Milwaukee ended its love affair with all things German, banning German newspapers and clubs and removing German poetry from its long-established place in the school curriculum.

With the death of William in 1917, the family moved to Washington, D.C., where Georgina obtained a government desk job more suited to her ability. Mildred spent her senior year with the offspring of diplomats and high-ranking politicians at a prestigious public high school. Between her literary and dramatic talents, she thrived. Two years later, however, she became homesick for the Midwest and transferred from George Washington University to the University of Wisconsin at Madison, the "city on a hill."

Mildred began her studies as a journalism major, writing arts reviews for the local *Wisconsin State Journal*. When she encountered the "glass ceiling" as the paper's society editor, she lost her zest for journalism and began focusing on endeavors more literary in nature. Mildred found her place on the editorial staff of the university's *Wisconsin Literary Magazine*, an organ of free thought and artistic experimentation then dominated by Kenneth Fearing and Margery Latimer, a stunning young woman from Portage who would become a respected modernist author. Mildred prospered in her studies of the classics; became a devotee of Walt Whitman and Ralph Waldo Emerson, with their depth, passion, and broad-mindedness; discovered the like-spirited German poet, Johann Wolfgang von Goethe; and when she graduated, took a position as lecturer in American literature.

It was from behind her lecture-hall podium that she first met her future husband, Arvid Harnack, a Rockefeller scholar from Germany. Arvid, a veteran of World War I, had gone on to complete one doctorate in law and was seeking another in economics. As fate would have it, he wandered into her undergraduate classroom by mistake.

After class he hastened to introduce himself to the young instructor whose intensity radiated through words whose English meanings he could not yet fully grasp.

The two spent long, luxurious springtime afternoons on and around the lakes surrounding campus, sharing flowers and poetry. Physically, they were a perfect "Aryan" match, both tall and fair: she slender and delicate-featured, he more robust. But it was their souls that complemented each other. They each had something to teach the other: English and poetry on her side, German and economics on his. Through his socialist ideology, her class-consciousness was channeled into an activist stance toward social issues. Despite their developing relationship, she enjoyed a large degree of independence. When they married in 1926, she took his name in hyphenated form, becoming Mildred Fish-Harnack.

The couple became regular "Friday niters" at the weekly gatherings among the elite leftist thinkers on campus, and frequently hosted these gatherings at their University Heights home. Madison was still the hub of the experiment in policy-making, started by Senator Robert M. La Follette who, along with his progressive stances on domestic issues, had opposed the Versailles Treaty ending World War I because of how it crippled Germany. The "Wisconsin Idea," as his philosophy became known, was simply the concept that government policy should be informed by the best economic and technical scholarship available. The scholars to provide these insights were the professors and graduate students with whom the young couple found themselves associated. These were heady times in Madison for all on the left, and for Mildred in particular, in whom love blossomed alongside intellectual development. She later referred to 1926 as "the one most beautiful year" of her life.

In 1927 Arvid's fellowship ended, forcing him to return to Germany, while Mildred fulfilled a one-year stint teaching at Goucher

College in Baltimore, close to her widowed mother. From there she applied for and won a fellowship enabling her to continue her literary studies in Germany. She arrived in the pastoral town of Jena, at a university where the great German figures of the Romantic period— Schiller, Schelling, Fichte, and Hegel—had taught. Arvid's family itself had a strong intellectual legacy and was closely connected to other families of great stature, including the Bonhoeffer family. Before she knew it, Mildred had fallen in love again, this time with Germany and its rich intellectual traditions.

Within two years of her arrival, Mildred saw Germany transformed. The country had limped through the 1920s, with economic sanctions imposed by the Treaty of Versailles hobbling the country's industry. The collapse of the American stock market in 1929 dramatically worsened the situation. Discontent became nothing less than desperation. When a long-discredited political party blamed "outsiders" for the nation's situation, people began to listen. In 1928 the Nazi party received less than 3 percent of the vote; by 1930 it was the second largest party in Germany with 18 percent of the vote. This movement toward fascism was even more pronounced in rural Germany, where Mildred was teaching.

Mildred and Arvid moved to Berlin just in time to witness the beginnings of the terror there. The summer of 1930 saw street violence by Nazi paramilitary "brown shirts." Their gains in the October election emboldened them further. In a letter to her mother, Mildred compared the National Socialists ("although it has nothing to do with socialism") to the American society of hatred, the Ku Klux Klan.

Her letters also describe the tattered and hungry-looking Germans she encountered, even in the halls of the University of Berlin. These pathetic apparitions convinced her that capitalism had run its course; the future, she felt, belonged to some other system. The Soviet Union was enjoying a rosy period in public relations, with Stalin's crimes still largely a secret. The extremism of the Nazis and the apparent failure of capitalism seen in the worldwide Depression seemed to call for an equal and opposite reaction. Furthermore, Soviet ideology was pro-feminist and pro-birth control—matters that deeply concerned Mildred. To top it off, the Soviet Union was at the time still exporting fine literature and film. Thus began Mildred's intellectual flirtation with Soviet communism.

In 1932 Arvid was invited along with other leaders of a Berlin study group on a trip to the Soviet Union. Mildred signed up for a shorter Intourist workers' package trip. The tour guides of both trips were careful to keep their visitors away from the suffering Russian masses, and both Harnacks found themselves rationalizing the cultural "backwardness" of the Russians they encountered. It was the status of women that most encouraged Mildred. Women could enter any field of endeavor they liked and enjoyed rights over their bodies and personal lives. She returned to Berlin with enthusiasm for the Soviet experiment.

Soon after she returned to Berlin, this enthusiasm was forced underground. When Hitler seized power in 1933, Communists were second only to Jews on the Nazi list of public enemies. Feeling unmoored, Mildred began socializing with Americans in Berlin, particularly those surrounding the ambassador's daughter, Martha Dodd, who earned a reputation for wild parties and romantic trysts. Mildred cherished the visit of the American novelist Thomas Wolfe with an intensity that belied her homesickness, and wrote some of her best literary criticism on his work. But she, like Wolfe, found that "You can't go home again." When, in 1937, she returned to the States in a half-hearted, yet desperate search for an academic post, she was radically changed from the lively woman she had once been. Her manner was so distant and her belief in communism so guarded that—with her cold Aryan features—many of her former friends assumed that she had become a closet Nazi. No doors opened, no friendships were rekindled, and she found herself back in Germany with even less direction than before.

For instance, like many women who lead academic, literary lives, she could not decide if she wanted to have children. In 1933, as the Nazis came to power with the slogan *Kinder, Kirche, Küche* (children, church, kitchen), the thirty-one-year-old Mildred found a doctor in England to perform an abortion. Perhaps it was their precarious finances that made her and Arvid reluctant to start a family; more likely, it was their horror of the Third Reich. It was not an auspicious time or place for children to enter the world. Four years later, however, Mildred found herself mourning a miscarriage. No longer a young woman, she saw life's opportunities slipping away from her.

Mildred's literary path was also uncertain. According to her biographer, her "creative" or non-academic writing displays no remarkable gift. She was, however, sensitive to language and literature and passionate about ideas: talents that would have taken her far as a literary critic and translator, in ordinary times. The Germany of the 1930s was by no means ordinary. Joseph Goebbels, Hitler's second in command, presided over the state cultural apparatus, which regulated publications and libraries; its purpose was to create, in Goebbels's words, "a cultural uniformity of the mind." One could not even purchase paper without being asked probing questions. In this climate, Mildred stopped writing literary criticism, concentrating her efforts on translations of German poetry.

What Mildred probably did best was teach. Her biography is filled with names of students who went on to become part of her salon. Soon, however, the literary character of the salons held at her apartment was transformed by the fatal undertow of the times: the more immediate and pressing concern of defeating Hitler. Mildred's literary activities and personal friendships became a cover for more subversive actions.

Over the years, Arvid had abandoned his outward interest in communism and instead developed a career in the state Economics Ministry. This was partly at the behest of his Soviet connections. In 1935 Arvid began to provide detailed information on the status of German currency, investments, and trade agreements to the Soviet Union, to America, and to the German resistance. As early as 1937, Mildred whispered intelligence to Martha Dodd in the embassy bathroom. After a more pointed recruitment by a Soviet agent in 1940, Arvid's communications were almost solely limited to contacts in the Soviet Union. The "orchestra" of spies to which he belonged developed an elaborate social web involving wives and children, so as to make their lives appear like those of ordinary, middle-class Germans.

It was to these dramas that Mildred ultimately sacrificed her life. In the words of the KGB file, she was "intelligent, sensitive, loyal, very much the German *Frau*, an intensely Nordic type and very useful." She tutored the children of spies in American litera-ture and took walks in parks in which documents were exchanged. She translated documents such as Roosevelt's and Churchill's speeches for the biweekly underground newspaper, *The Inner Front*, which her circle established. She recruited at least four of her stu-dents. Even as British bombs fell in Berlin, she moderated discus-sions, not on literature as it might have appeared to outsiders, but on socialist principles, to help the group prepare for the day when a coup against Hitler succeeded.

Arvid never asked for nor received money for this work. He and Mildred aided the Soviet Union in the belief that it was Ger-many's best hope for defeating Hitler. In this way they were unique. They were not agents of another country. Arvid was German to the core and felt he was serving his country. But Mildred's motives were more complex. Was it love of her husband or love of her adoptive country that moved her? At one point in the buildup to war, Arvid purchased Mildred a one-way steamer ticket to America. Mildred had declined his offer.

Mildred's involvement went further than mere loyalty. Her "bit part" on the grand stage of world history belonged to her. Mildred, with her sober personality, would never have asked for such a role; she was not intoxicated by danger and excitement, as others were. Her sacrifice was most of all to the ideal of the individual, celebrated in the writings of her most cherished Romantic authors, the American essayist Emerson and the German poet Goethe.

Mildred lived just long enough to learn of the German surrender at Stalingrad, considered by many the turning point of World War II. The Red Orchestra is said to have provided the intelligence that helped the Soviets gain the advantage through the long winter siege. Whether or not this legend is true, it is certain that Mildred paid for Hitler's loss with her life. Initially sentenced to only six years in prison by the court, this courageous American woman became a scapegoat upon whom the *führer* exerted his infernal wrath.

The imminence of death brought a kind of clarity to Mildred's life's journey. In the weeks before their trial, Arvid wrote her a letter full of love and the joyful memories they had shared. He quoted Walt Whitman, just as she would copy out poems by Goethe in her final days. In the letter's finest passage, he wrote, "Our intense work meant that life was not easy for us. . . . Nonetheless, we remained human beings. This became clear to me during our time [in the Alps], and again this year, as we watched the great elk emerge before us. Earlier, you had risen from the sea like a goddess."

The five days of the trial would be the last that Mildred and Arvid spent together. Certain of a death sentence, Arvid spoke plainly about his economic views and his hatred for the Third Reich. Mildred answered a series of "yes" and "no" questions, then left the room while witnesses were called on her behalf. They portrayed her sympathetically as a "highly educated American" and a lover of German culture; after all, she had translated many important German works into English. Despite her literary accomplishments, the Nazi ideology of women's intellectual limitations allowed her lawyer to float the notion that her grasp of German politics was naive and uninformed. Rather, he asserted, her involvement had been guided by wifely devotion. Attempting to save her life, Arvid accepted full blame for drawing her into this treasonous web. When her sentence was read, his face beamed with joy; her life had been spared.

Arvid was hanged three days before Christmas of 1942 with the belief that his wife would live. Soon after, Hitler demanded a retrial for Mildred and another woman who had avoided execution.

The second trial featured salacious lies: Mildred was accused of attempting to seduce a German official for the purpose of gaining access to government secrets. It is likely that Mildred incriminated herself in the second trial by admitting the much more mundane facts. She had nothing to live for, no husband beaming confidently from the courtroom benches. Within six months she had changed from "goddess" to a frail, white-haired woman, wracked with tuberculosis.

Mildred spent her last days in prison teaching her cellmate American songs and writing out snatches of remembered poetry on the cell walls. She had talked endlessly about her days with Arvid, about their "one most beautiful year." In the hour before her death, she gave her treasured book on the classics, authored by one of her University of Wisconsin professors, to the female prison guard who stood watch as she prepared herself for the guillotine. Mildred was one of nineteen women of the Red Orchestra who were executed.

In 1979 a secondary school in East Berlin was named after Mildred. In 1986 the Wisconsin legislature established her birthday,

September 16, as a day of annual remembrance. Mildred would be glad to know that young people in both of her homes remember her name, her works, and her spirit.

BIBLIOGRAPHY

QUEEN MARINETTE

Austin, H. Russell. *The Wisconsin Story: The Building of a Vanguard State.* 1948. Reprint, Milwaukee: The Journal Company, 1964.

Johnson, Beverly Hayward. *Queen Marinette: Spirit of Survival on the Great Lakes Frontier.* Amasa, Mich.: White Water Associates, Inc., 1995.

Rentmeester, Jeanne, and Les Rentmeester. *The Wisconsin Creoles.* Melbourne, Fla.: Jeanne and Les Rentmeester, 1987.

Wyman, Mark. *The Wisconsin Frontier.* Bloomington: Indiana University Press, 1998.

ELIZA CHAPPELL PORTER

Finney, Charles G. *The Autobiography of Charles G. Finney.* 1876. Edited by Helen S. Wessel. Reprint, Minneapolis: Bethany House Publishers, 1977.

Harkenrider, Zach. "Introduction to Charles Grandison Finney's Letter." *American Intellectual History* 267 (April 1999). Online: www.lib.rochester .edu/rbk/Finneyessay.htm

Pferdehirt, Julia. *Freedom Train North: Stories of the Underground Railroad in Wisconsin.* Seattle: Living History Press, 1999.

Porter, Mary H. *Eliza Chappell Porter: A Memoir.* Chicago: Fleming H. Revell Co., 1892.

CORDELIA A. P. HARVEY

Bauchle, May L. "The Shopiere Shrine." *Wisconsin Magazine of History* 10,1 (September 1926): 29–34.

"Cordelia Adelaide Perrine." Talvacchio Family Genealogy. Online: home.earthlink.net/~talvacchio/index.html

Crandell, Ralph J. "New England's Migration Fever: The Expansion of America." *Ancestry Magazine* (July 2000). Online: www.ancestry.com/ library/view/ancmag/2834.asp

1st Wisconsin Cavalry Reeanactment Organization. "Unit History."
Online: www.1stwisconsincav.org/WrittenCavHistory.htm

Harrsch, Patricia G. " 'This Noble Monument': The Story of the Soldiers'
Orphans' Home." *Wisconsin Magazine of History* 76, 2 (Winter 1992–93):
82–120.

Harvey, Cordelia A. P. "A Wisconsin Woman's Picture of President Lincoln."
Wisconsin Magazine of History 1,3 (March 1918): 233–55.

Harvey, Cordelia A. P. Letters. *Wisconsin Electronic Reader*. Online: www
.library.wisc.edu/etext/wireader/WER1620-1.html

Harvey, Cordelia A. P. Letters. *Wisconsin Goes to War: Digital Civil War
Collections.* Online: www.uwosh.edu/archives/civilwar/civilwar.html

McKinney, Mrs. William. "Mrs. Cordelia A. P. Harvey" In *Sketches of Wisconsin
Pioneer Women,* edited by Florence Dexheimer, 47–49. Fort Atkinson, Wis.:
Hoard and Sons, 1924.

National Park Service. "Medicine in the Civil War." Online: www.nps.gov/
gett/gettkidz/doctor.htm

MARGARETHE MEYER SCHURZ

Baylor, Ruth M. *Elizabeth Palmer Peabody: Kindergarten Pioneer.* Philadelphia:
Temple University Press, 1965.

Froebel, Friedrich. *Pedagogics of the Kindergarten.* Translated by Josephine
Jarvis. New York: Appleton & Co., 1904.

Jenkins, Elizabeth. "How the Kindergarten Found Its Way to America."
Wisconsin Magazine of History 14,1 (September 1930): 46–62.

Peabody, Elizabeth P. "Origin and Growth of the Kindergarten." *Education*
2 (May–June 1882): 510–27.

Schurz, Carl. *Reminiscences of Carl Schurz.* 3 vols. New York: The McClure
Company, 1907–1908.

Swart, Hannah Werwarth. *Margarethe Meyer Schurz.* Watertown, Wis.: Watertown
Historical Society, 1967.

Trefousse, Hans L. *Carl Schurz: A Biography.* Knoxville: University of Tennessee
Press, 1982.

BIBLIOGRAPHY

BELLE CASE LA FOLLETTE

Freeman, Lucy, Sherry La Follette, and George A. Zabriskie. *Belle: The Biography of Belle Case La Follette*. New York: Beaufort Books, 1986.

La Follette, Belle Case, and Fola La Follette. *Robert M. La Follette*. New York: The Macmillan Company, 1953.

Maney, Patrick. *Young Bob: A Biography of Robert M. La Follette, Jr.* 2nd ed. Madison: University of Wisconsin Press, 2002.

Schultze, Steve. "La Follette Death Linked to Fear of McCarthy." *Milwaukee Journal Sentinal*, May 18, 2003.

Unger, Nancy. "The Two Worlds of Belle Case La Follette." *Wisconsin Magazine of History* 83, 2 (Winter 1999/2000): 82–110.

Weisberger, Bernard A. *The La Follettes of Wisconsin: Love and Politics in Progressive America*. Madison: University of Wisconsin Press, 1994.

HARRIET BELL MERRILL

Bastien, Joseph. *The Kiss of Death: Chagas' Disease in the Americas*. Austin: University of Texas at Austin, 1998. Online: www.uta.edu/chagas

Goc, Michael J. *Land and Lumber, a History of Portage County*. Friendship, Wis.: New Past Press, 1999.

Hartridge, Merrilyn L. *The Anandrous Journey: Revealing Letters to a Mentor*. Amherst, Wis.: Palmer Publications, 1997.

Hartridge, Merrilyn L. "H. B. Merrill: Early Wisconsin Scientist and Adventurer." *Wisconsin Academy Review* 41, 2 (Spring 1995): 16–22.

Kipling, Rudyard. *Just So Stories*. London: Macmillan, 1902.

Rowe, C. L. and Hebert, P.D.N. Cladoceran Web Site. University of Guelph. 1999. Online: www.cladocera.uoguelph.ca

LILLIE ROSA MINOKA-HILL

Apple, Rima D. "Lillie Rosa Minoka-Hill." *Women and Health* 4, 4 (Winter 1979): 329–31.

"Beloved Physician Adopted by Tribe." *Milwaukee Sentinel*, November 28, 1947.

Hill, Roberta Jean. "Dr. Lillie Rosa Minoka-Hill: Mohawk Woman Physician." Ph.D. diss., University of Minnesota, 1998. 2 vols.

Malinsky, Barbara. "The (Women's) Medical College of Philadelphia." *Women and Health* 4, 3 (Fall 1979): 217–21.

Rogow, Sally. "Indian Doctor: Rosa Minoka Hill, M.D." Unpublished manuscript in Special Collections of the Wisconsin State Historical Society, Green Bay branch, 1969.

ELSA ULBRICHT

Bates, Kirk. "A Project That Made Milwaukee Famous." *Milwaukee Journal*, May 26, 1944.

Ehrlich, Howard. "The Milwaukee W.P.A. Handicrafts Project." Tape-recorded interview with Elsa Ulbricht, June 11, 1964. Transcript, 37 pages, in Golda Meir Library, University of Wisconsin–Milwaukee.

Harney, Andy Leon. "WPA Handicrafts Rediscovered." *Historic Preservation* 25, 3 (July–September, 1973): 10–15.

Merrill, Peter C. "Elsa Ulbricht: A Career in Art," *Milwaukee History* 16, 1 (Spring 1993): 22–28. Online: www.tfaoi.com/aa/3aa/3aa88.htm

Quinn, Lois M., John Pawasarat, and Laura Serebin. "WPA Milwaukee Handicraft Project." In *History of Jobs for Workers on Relief in Milwaukee County, 1930–1994.* Milwaukee: University of Wisconsin–Milwaukee Employment and Training Institute, 1995. Online: www.uwm.edu/Dept/ETI/wpamilw.htm

Sanders, Barry. *A Complex Fate: Gustav Stickley and the Craftsman Movement.* Washington, D.C.: Preservation Press, 1996.

Ulbricht, Elsa. Archives. Golda Meir Library, University of Wisconsin–Milwaukee.

Wisconsin Designer Crafts Council. "A Rich History." July 16, 2003. Online: www.wdcc.org/about/history.html

EDNA FERBER

Ferber, Edna. *A Peculiar Treasure.* New York: Doubleday, Duran, 1939.

———. *A Kind of Magic.* New York: Doubleday, 1963.

———. *Emma McChesney & Co.* New York: Grosset & Dunlap, 1915.

———. *So Big.* New York: Doubleday, Page, 1924.

Gilbert, Julie Goldsmith. *Edna Ferber and Her Circle of Friends*. Garden City, N.Y.: Doubleday, 1978.

MABEL WATSON RAIMEY

Menard, Maggie. "Decisions: The Law Lives of Four Women." *Milwaukee Sentinel*, February 15, 1984, 6.

Muchka, Albert. Assistant Curator/Collections Manager—History, Milwaukee Public Museum. Conversation with author, July 28, 2003.

————. "Thirty Dollars Down and a Lifetime to Buy: The Watson Raimey Collection." *Lore* 43, 4 (December 1993): 5–9. Online: www.mpm.edu/collect/black_history/blhist.html

Raimey, Mabel Watson. Vertical File. Marquette University Archives. The John P. Raynor, S.J., Library.

State Historical Society of Wisconsin. "Milwaukee Urban League." *Archives: Finding Aid*. Online: www.uwm.edu/Library/arch/findaids/mssez.htm

Thomson, William F. *History of Wisconsin, Vol. 6: Continuity and Change, 1940–1965*. Madison: State Historical Society of Wisconsin, 1988.

Trotter, Joe William, Jr. *Black Milwaukee: The Making of an Industrial Proletariat, 1915–1945*. Urbana: University of Illinois Press, 1985.

Williams, Phoebe Weaver. "A Black Woman's Voice: The Story of Mabel Raimey, 'Shero,' " *Marquette Law Review* 74 (Winter 1991–92) 345–76.

Zaniewski, Kazimierz J., and Carol J. Rosen. *The Atlas of Ethnic Diversity in Wisconsin*. Madison: University of Wisconsin Press, 1998.

GOLDA MEIR

Martin, Ralph. *Golda: Golda Meir, the Romantic Years*. New York: Charles Scribner's Sons, 1988.

Meir, Golda. *Golda Meir Speaks Out*. London: Weidenfeld and Nicolson, 1973.

Meir, Golda. *My Life*. New York: G. P. Putnam's Sons, 1975.

Morris, Terry. *Shalom, Golda*. New York: Hawthorne Books, Inc., 1971.

Roosevelt, Eleanor. "Foreword." *This is Our Strength: Selected Papers of Golda Meir*. New York: Macmillan, 1962.

More than Petticoats

MILDRED FISH-HARNACK

Brysac, Shareen Blair. *Resisting Hitler: Mildred Harnack and the Red Orchestra*. New York: Oxford University Press, 2000.

Florida Center for Instructional Technology. "A Teacher's Guide to the Holocaust." 2001. Online: fcit.coedu.usf.edu/holocaust/timeline/timeline.htm

Garson, Sandra. "Better Not Write but Don't Forget Me." *Wisconsin Alumnus* 87 (May–June 1986): 8–12. Online: digital.library.wisc.edu/1711.dl/UW.v87i4

Tarrant, V. E. *The Red Orchestra: The Soviet Spy Network Inside Nazi Europe*. New York: Sterling Publishers 1999.

ℐNDEX

Index

Index

About the Author

Greta Anderson grew up in Columbus, Ohio, and lived in California, Massachusetts, and New Jersey before finding a home in Iowa City, Iowa. She currently works as a freelance writer and editor while teaching writing at Kirkwood Community College in Cedar Rapids. She is the author of *More than Petticoats: Remarkable Texas Women.*